A Northern Tale

by

John Entwhistle

A Northern Tale

ISBN **978-0-9560191-8-9**

Published by Ragged Cover Publishing
http://www.raggedcover.com

for Dominant Designs
http://www.dominantdesigns.co.uk

Cover Design & Illustration by Mark Frain
Awesome Creative
http://www.awesomecreative.co.uk

A set of colour illustrations may be downloaded from
http://www.dominantdesigns.co.uk
Or email: pictures@dominantdesigns.co.uk

An Interesting Friday

John found an empty compartment and threw his suitcase on to the overhead rack. He slumped down in the corner seat and opened his newspaper. He did not expect to be on his own for long and didn't want any contact with anyone else. He just wanted time to think.

Here he was at the age of 19 on his way to report for National Service. Five years before he had left school as an under-educated and undernourished war child. Now he was on his way to learn to be a man and hopefully an officer and a gentleman.

In between he had been a girl and a young woman. He had experienced a taste of a life of luxury and had an insight into the world of high fashion rubberised rainwear, beyond the imagining of someone from his humble origins. Now this whirlwind experience was finally over. The best way to describe how he felt was numb! He just wanted time to think and find himself.

It had all started one cold Friday afternoon in January nearly four years before. But let John tell you his story himself.

***

Many towns in Lancashire were built high up in the valleys to harness the water power for the early textile mills. The communities that grew up around the mills stayed even though cotton spinning and weaving moved to the plains of Lancashire with the coming of steam power.

Brunley was one such town which stayed up in the valleys after the cotton industry had gone. It was where I was born, some years before the Second World War. Despite the difficulties of the thirties, my parents always found work and provided well for us. They had four children of whom I was the eldest. Like most eldest boys, I was called John.

I was an only child for five years but then my parents got busy. They had four more children in quick succession. Sadly one of them died. Then my father 'went to war' and didn't come back.

I don't have very good childhood memories. I just remember it being cold, grim and boring. My mother worked long hours and I had to help my grandmother to look after my brothers and sister. My education was perfunctory. My mother was tough. She had to be. She made sure I attended the local school during the war, unless there was a genuine family crisis and then I had to stay at home to help.

Even after the war had ended things were still very grim. We had rationing and power cuts and I seemed to be hungry most of the time. Although I was tall for my age, I remember that I was excruciatingly thin.

One winter Friday afternoon, when I was 14, I saw my mother through the classroom window coming into the school. At first I wondered if there was trouble but I couldn't think of anything I had done wrong recently. Then I had the consoling thought that something interesting was likely to happen to break the monotony of tedious lessons.

Sure enough, a few minutes later I was summoned to the Headmaster's office and told to wait outside.

Not long after the door opened and my mother came out. She looked quite cheerful.

"Get your things together," she said, "you are leaving school."

As we walked home she told me that as I would be 15 next term, I could then officially leave school. She had told Mr. Higginbottom, the Headmaster, that she could not afford to wait until then for me to start work. She had got a job for me to start next week.

"The money won't be much to start with," she said,

"but it will help."

I said nothing but thought this must be the interesting thing I had foreseen.

"Don't you want to know where you are going to work?" asked my mother.

"Yes," I said.

"Well, you will be a tea boy at Atkinson's raincoat factory on ten shillings a week."

I was able to express sincere delight to my mother at the idea of being free of school and going to work. I had had a variety of jobs, delivering newspapers and working in shops behind the scenes, but this was different. It was the prospect of working full-time and imminent adulthood.

This was very convenient because inside there was another feeling. It was all I could do to stop from blushing. I pretended indifference to the prospect of working at Atkinson's but inside my heart was racing.

Ever since being about seven, I had been aware that ladies wore different clothes to men and these intrigued me. Most particularly I liked clothes that made noises. I found especially fascinating the raincoats that ladies wore that had smooth rubber linings.

Sometimes my mother took me with her to the centre of Brunley. Money was always short but her occasional pleasure was to go to the only department store in town for tea. My mother was a great dreamer so the trip included going into every department looking at things she could not afford. Much of it was dull but when we went to the Ladies' Fashion Department I had to pretend indifference. I was a little intimidated by the snooty women who worked there and who spoke in false accents, like voices on the radio.

My mother knew some of the ladies who worked there because they had been at school together. I realise now that she must have been very well liked at school. They all made a fuss of her and must have sympathised with her being a war widow, something that could have happened to any of them. If it was quiet they would encourage her to try on clothes and I would sit on a chair as she paraded them. They used to tease me by asking my opinion. Of course it was always favourable and it was nice to see my mother in bright clothes by comparison to what she had to wear the rest of the time.

Sometimes she would try on raincoats. Of course she and I knew that there was no possibility that she could afford to buy one. Still, we used to play the game of choosing which one she would buy when she became rich. She always thought she would!

I had picked up the information that some of these wonderful raincoats were made here in Brunley by a firm called Atkinson's. I even knew where the factory was located. It was out of the way up the valley, on a bus route that went up into the hill villages. It was a grim black building that must have been an old textile mill originally.

So it was with some pleasant expectations that I started out at 7am on the following Monday to my first day's work at Atkinson's!

The First Meeting

It was quite a bright morning when I climbed the hill to Atkinson's on my first day there. Even though I had to come a little later than the usual start time, the office was not yet open. I had to ask for Mr. Wilkinson and was directed to a side entrance which opened into the yard. This was the dispatch department and it was where I was to spend quite some time.

Mr. Wilkinson was one of those old company servants who seemed as old as Methuselah when I first met him. He had worked at Atkinson's ever since he returned from the First World War. I was to learn much about life from him and in some ways he probably filled the gap left by my father. Only many years later did I learn his first name was William because he was universally known as Mr. Wilkinson.

The foolish ideas that I had about spending my days examining the insides of fashionable ladies' raincoats and smelling their delicious odour were soon dispelled.

Instead, I spent my days at the beck and call of half a dozen strong-minded and strong-mouthed women. These ladies were referred to as 'girls' by Mr. Wilkinson and themselves. I was allowed to call them by their first names but I could never think of them as girls. They were all much the same age and character as my mother. In fact a number of them knew my mother so I knew any cheek or indiscretions would be reported back and I would soon hear about it from her.

It was not that my mother was brutal with me. She said I was the head of the family now and she relied on me to give her the help and support she needed with the younger family. Any lapse on my part was portrayed in a way that created shame and guilt in me. The last thing I wanted was her to hear of my furtive interest in ladies' clothing, especially rainwear. I felt guilty enough about that already.

My time was spent on the periphery of the vital function of packing and dispatch. The six girls would receive the magnificent finished rainwear on hangers from the warehouse. These items had been selected to meet the orders taken from the shops that our sales representatives had called upon.

The girls would check the garments against the paperwork. They would then wrap them in tissue paper and fold them with great skill into cardboard boxes, which were lined with more tissue paper.

My job was to keep the girls supplied with cardboard boxes, sheets of tissue paper, rolls of string, sealing wax, pencils and the other things they needed. In those days finished garments were sent out to the retail shops in rectangular collapsible cardboard boxes. The boxes could hold between one and four garments and each one had a card on which was written the name and address of the retail customer and the contents of the box.

Most of the deliveries went by British Railways. They sent a lorry every day which I recall was a trailer pulled by a three-wheel tractor unit. It came at about 4.30 each afternoon. The lorry would not wait and it was vital that everything was ready when it came. This was when I had to fly into action. Previously Mr. Wilkinson did this on his own but now business was expanding and it was getting too much for him to do.

When the lorry arrived, the first thing to be done was to unload the returned boxes. These came back flattened and tied in bundles with string. The bundles had to be taken from the lorry and stacked in the corner. Then the filled boxes, each tied with string and sealed with sealing wax, were loaded from trolleys into the back of the lorry trailer. My job was to make sure everything was ready for the lorry. I had to make sure all the boxes for loading agreed with the paperwork that the driver would sign.

My only consolation was writing and saying the glamorous style names and colours. I remember 'Paris Spring' in Dark Cherry and 'Roman Holiday' in Antique Gold. My closest contact with these exotic garments was to imagine them inside the sturdy cardboard boxes I was loading onto the lorry.

Another part of my job was to inspect the returned boxes, outside and inside, and re-line them with brown paper. Atkinson's prided itself not just on the quality and style of its raincoats but also on every aspect of its presentation. This included the appearance of the boxes in which the garments were sent out.

These boxes were dark green and had the name Atkinson's emblazoned in gold on the lid. I quickly learned from Mr. Wilkinson what was the required condition in which a box could be re-used and which were too battered to use again. I also had to check the cardholders and if necessary replace them. In addition I had to have a stock of new boxes made-up ready to be used for the first time.

I had to supply each of the six girls with enough lined boxes for their needs. They worked at long benches with their rails of garments, covered in brown paper shrouds to protect the garments from dust, next to them. I came to the other side of the benches with empty boxes and removed those that were filled and checked and took the appropriate paperwork. I had to stay ahead all day otherwise they would shout at me.

All I saw and touched were empty boxes, string, cardboard labels and filled, sealed boxes, the contents of which I could only fantasies about. Just occasionally I saw a raincoat lying open on a bench while being inspected but I did not dare dawdle to look at it or someone might have guessed my guilty secret.

Then half an hour before the break I had to put on the big kettle and make the tea. Just before the hooter went for the tea-break, I had to pour the tea into the designated cups with the right amount of sugar in each. The 15-minute tea-break was extremely precious and each girl wanted her tea ready to her taste to drink with her cigarette.

I did not have my tea-break at that time as it was a good time to get all the girls stocked up with boxes, to buy me a bit of breathing space to do the other jobs I had to do. Sometimes during the tea-breaks I would see a selection of beautiful raincoats waiting to be packed on one of the rails that had its shroud temporarily removed. However I was still within view of the girls and the most I could do was give them a second glance.

The girls checked each others' cards before the boxes were tied with string and then sealed with sealing wax. I had to check the listed contents of each box against the overall delivery docket for each particular customer and number the boxes according to the docket.

The usual pattern was that Mr. Wilkinson went to the office early in the afternoon and got copies of the orders that came in from our travellers which had to be despatched the next day. The same orders went to the finished goods warehouse and they selected the goods from stock to fill the orders. Our packers had to check the garments were what they were supposed to be and that there were no marks or blemishes on them.

It was a good system and worked well. Nevertheless Mr. Wilkinson was always anxious that everything was running as it should be. If customers did not get their delivery on time or they said it was not right, Mr. Wilkinson was called to the office to explain to Mrs. Atkinson what had gone wrong.

Business was brisk that summer and we were fully stretched every day. However Mr. Wilkinson lived in fear of a message from the office asking him to go and see Mrs. Atkinson. When he came back with the offending paperwork and a white face, he would conduct an investigation of what had happened to that particular order. I had a picture of Mrs. Atkinson as a real dragon. She must have been one to put such fear into Mr. Wilkinson.

And so I spent my early months at Atkinson's. I was pleased to be busy and to be taking home ten shillings a week to my mother. I was well organised and within a few weeks had a system going so I always had a stock of boxes checked and ready.

I used to come in ten or fifteen minutes early to start getting my boxes out on the benches for the first orders. Sometimes I got in before Mr. Wilkinson but the gatekeeper had instructions to let me in.

One wet and windy morning I was in early, carrying a pile of boxes to the benches, when I heard the door open behind me. I thought it was Mr. Wilkinson or one of the girls. Then I heard a swishing noise and the door bang closed. I looked round and saw a tall lady wearing a magnificent long raincoat.

It was silver in colour and obviously rubber-lined. The long line of the raincoat was billowed out from her bust. The raincoat came down to just above her ankles. It was buttoned all the way up to her neck.

This wonderful coat was topped with a generous hood that was held in place with a bow just in front of her chin. There were dark grey spatters of rain on the coat and hood but enough of the fabric was dry to show definite silver glints. These caught the light as she shook out the skirts of the coat so the surface rain fell to the floor.

I was so shocked that I stumbled and put down the boxes on the first available surface.

From inside the hood came the words, "Good morning. Is Mr. Wilkinson here yet?"

Now I could see a bit better into the hood. I saw a pair of beautiful dark eyes, a strong nose and full red lips. I even suspected I saw a glint of amusement in her eyes at my obvious confusion.

I mumbled something about being sure Mr. Wilkinson would not be very long and prayed a silent prayer that he would come soon.

Now from inside the hood came a gentle hum of recognition and the words, "So you must be Alice Entwhistle's boy. John isn't it?"

I muttered some confirmation but was hit by the fact she used my mother's maiden name. Was there no getting away from people who knew my mother?

This was quickly followed by a feeling of absolute horror! She put out an exquisitely gloved hand in my direction.

"I am Glynis Atkinson," she said.

I had barely touched the black leather of her glove when the door opened and in bustled Mr. Wilkinson, much to my intense relief.

"Good morning Mr. Wilkinson. I know I am early but this is a very important showing and the journey into Manchester may take longer than usual in this weather. Are my show garments ready?"

"Oh yes Mrs. Atkinson. I'll bring them to your car."

"I am sure John here can take care of that," replied Mrs. Atkinson.

"John, go to my office," said Mr. Wilkinson, "and on the bench at the side you will find three Atkinson's boxes. Bring them here for Mrs. Atkinson."

I was pleased to get out of the room for a few

seconds. I found the boxes and now had something to hide behind.

Mr. Wilkinson opened the door for Mrs. Atkinson and she stepped lightly through it carrying her car keys. I fell in behind with my burden of the three boxes.

I followed her across the yard to where a glistening car was standing. She went to the back of the car and I was delighted to follow that glamorous figure in its magnificent swishing raincoat.

She opened the car boot and stood back. I placed the boxes in the boot and pulled down the boot lid. She stepped forward and locked it.

"Thank you," she said from inside her big hood. Her voice was deep for a lady but her speech was clear and light. It had a strange musical quality.

"Now you had better get back inside, before you catch your death of cold."

I was glad to get away and ran back inside. Only then did I realise my overall was soaked through. But also I had a worry. Should I have stayed and held the door open for her?

"So now you have met Mrs. Atkinson for the first time," said Mr. Wilkinson.

"Oh yes" I said nonchalantly, but my thoughts were in turmoil.

3

The Real Mrs. Atkinson

Glynis Atkinson was a local girl and the daughter of a shopkeeper. Surprisingly her father was French. Nobody knew how a Frenchman came to be living in Brunley and owning a business there. Her parents could afford to send her to train as a secretary in Manchester in the 1920s and later she went to Paris to work. On a trip back to Brunley she had met Tom Atkinson who was the son of the original founder of the company, Albert Atkinson. Tom and Glynis married in the early 1930s.

During the Second World War, Atkinson's had made military clothing and equipment that was made from rubberised fabric. Tom Atkinson had trained as a rubber chemist and engineer and by the beginning of the war was jointly running Atkinson's with his father. He was not called up because he was needed to ensure the new products being developed were able to meet the needs of the military. As the war progressed he became more and more drawn into organising military supplies. He was away a lot of the time and was eventually seconded as a civil servant for the duration of the war. During this time Glynis had taken an active part in running the company with her father-in-law.

As I learned from Mr. Wilkinson the pressure on people concerned with supplying the war effort was as bad as on those who were actively fighting. Sadly the demands had affected Mr. Tom's health and he came back after the war an ailing man. He died soon after of tuberculosis.

As Atkinson's switched back to producing civilian rainwear, they naturally reverted to the fashions of the time.

These were short above-the-knee coats to go with the short skirt lengths that ladies had worn during the war. These were usually made in dull colours in keeping with the post-war atmosphere of continuing austerity. It was a time of drabness. Clothes were drab and so was rainwear.

Then in 1947 Christian Dior had shocked the world with the New Look. Suddenly hemlines dropped from above the knee to halfway down the calf.

It was due to Glynis's good judgment that Atkinson's switched over to the new longer-length coats in the late 40s and started to use more colourful fabrics. It was her belief that ladies raincoats would now move from being utility garments that kept the rain off to high fashion garments that would be worn on the catwalks of the world. This meant they would cost more to make but customers would be willing to pay more for them. She was right!

Mr. Wilkinson explained to me that this fashion change to the New Look had had quite an effect on the pattern of the business over recent years. Originally these fashion changes started in Paris and took time to spread around the world. Even then such follies were reserved for the wealthy minority who could afford to buy copies of Paris originals. However by the early 50s prosperity was beginning to return and ladies could afford to indulge themselves occasionally. Even at the higher price, a fashionable raincoat in a strong colour was an affordable indulgence. Fashion rainwear was moving towards the mass market! Atkinson's was one of the pioneers of fashion raincoats in England and we were riding the wave with booming sales.

I readjusted my calendar from the day I first met Mrs. Atkinson! I counted the days and the weeks from that date. I had hardly seen her face but it was the combination of her commanding presence and that beautiful silver raincoat. Amazingly that coat was to become mine in years to come!

I took every opportunity to get Mr. Wilkinson talking about the history of Atkinson's and I was pleased to get him talking about Mrs. Atkinson. It transpired that she worked irregular hours because she had to look after old Mrs. Atkinson who was now bedridden. They lived in the big house that had been the family home for many years. Mr. Albert Atkinson had died during the war and the other son had gone missing in action and his body had never been found. They had been a sad family and now all that was left were the two Mrs. Atkinson's. There were other relatives on old Mrs. Atkinson's side but Mr. Albert had always kept them away from the business. Nevertheless it was rumoured that some of them were nominally on the payroll.

I once mentioned it was a shame Tom and Glynis had not had children. Mr. Wilkinson became very somber and said that they might have had and made it very clear that he did not want to be asked any more about it.

I realised now that it was not that Mrs. Atkinson was a dragon who made Mr. Wilkinson's life a misery. It was that Mr. Wilkinson came from that very deferential generation who believed that the boss was right in all things and everything had to be done right for them. Actually I found out later that Mrs. Atkinson had a great affection for Mr. Wilkinson and valued his advice in a number of areas of the business.

From the time of that first meeting, I kept my eyes very much open to see Mrs. Atkinson again. There weren't many private cars in the yard but now I knew hers and I knew where she parked it. She came at different times in the morning and was often still there when I went home.

I could see her car parking space from the window of the packing room where my bench was. I would watch for her arrival when I could do so without the risk of rebuke by Mr. Wilkinson, or worse still, any of the girls.

I noticed that she wore a series of different raincoats

on days when there was a cloud in the sky. I suppose that was good for business. If Mrs. Atkinson wore the company products then the rest of the world would follow suit.

I didn't see the magnificent silver coat again but she had a number of regulars in Cherry Red, Dusk Blue and Autumn Gold. They were all in the fashionable length and shape that Mr. Wilkinson had told me about. I knew my colours from the delivery notes but could only guess at the styles. Some had belts and some were shaped to go into a very small waist. Some had big collars and others had hoods. Whenever it was rainy, as it often was in Brunley, I would be speculating which of her lovely raincoats Mrs. Atkinson would be wearing that day.

When it was fine she would be dressed smartly in a long skirt and short, shapely jacket. She was of the generation who always wore a hat. Sometimes it was a big glamorous hat like Greta Garbo used to wear, sometimes a small hat with a feather and sometimes a beret. When she wore the beret she looked quite continental. Once I knew about her French father and that she had worked in France I realised that was the source of her elegance and good taste in clothes.

Occasionally Mr. Wilkinson would send me upstairs to the office to deliver some papers to Mrs. Atkinson. If she was in the outer office, it gave me a chance to observe her more closely than from the packing room window. She was always very well made-up and wore her hair up and off her neck. She had a strong profile and mouth. She had piercing but not unkind eyes.

She was very welcoming to me. She always asked how my mother was and about my sister and brothers. She thanked me for what I had brought and sent me back promptly, saying she was sure Mr. Wilkinson had plenty for me to do. Sometimes I could see through her open office door and there would be the raincoat of the day adorning the coat stand just inside the door.

When she was in her inner office with the door closed, it was a different story. The door was guarded by a woman who I suppose was her secretary. To me she seemed as old as time and she greeted me with a fierce glare. She told me to put the papers down on her desk and get back to my work. I remembered that I had occasionally seen her appear in the packing department to get something from Mr. Wilkinson. Originally I must have thought that she was the Mrs. Atkinson he referred to in such deferential terms.

4

The Visit

So I worked through the summer and into the autumn. We were so busy that our department worked on through the annual shutdown. It didn't matter to me because I had not been there long enough to be entitled to holiday pay and my mother needed the money.

My fifteenth birthday came and went and I was beginning to get restless. The novelty of working so close to such lovely raincoats was wearing off and I had my job very much under control. The only bright thing was the occasional encounter with the glamorous Mrs. Atkinson. She summed up for me all the exotic appeal of the world outside Brunley that I felt was passing me by. Was it time to try to better myself?

My mother was not sympathetic. Job security was the paramount thing in her mind and she was only just beginning to get in control financially. Then she told me that Mrs. Atkinson had had very good reports about me from Mr. Wilkinson. Whilst I was flattered, I was still annoyed at all these people watching me and exchanging comments. Also it told me that my mother and Glynis Atkinson were in communication. This would be another line back to my mother if my guilty secret was ever exposed at Atkinson's.

Then one day Mr. Wilkinson called me into his office. "I want you to get well ahead with your boxes by dinner-time so you can go on an errand for me during the break."

"But what about my dinner, Mr. Wilkinson?" I said.

"You can take it with you and eat it on the bus. Just make sure the guard doesn't see you."

He made it clear by his tone that he was not able to say more at that stage.

All morning I was wondering what rare adventure awaited me. In the late morning someone from the factory brought in one of our Atkinson's boxes already tied up with string and took it into Mr. Wilkinson's office. I wondered if it was anything to do with my mission as I built my mountain of boxes.

Just before dinner Mr. Wilkinson called me into his office. He explained that Mrs. Atkinson Senior had been taken bad and our Mrs. Atkinson had to stay at home. She had been waiting for a new design raincoat from the workroom and it had only just been finished. She wanted it taken up to her at the house so she could check it.

I was to take it to Mrs. Atkinson and wait to bring it back with a note of any modifications she wanted. He gave me the address and money for the bus fare. He told me which bus to catch from the central bus station and where to ask to be put off. In a rush and with my hidden excitement at the prospect of an encounter with Mrs. Atkinson, I forgot my sandwiches!

On the bus I clutched my parcel close to me as if it were the crown jewels. I sat as close to the guard as I could so that I should not miss the instruction of when to get off. Eventually we got there. It was in the upper part of town, close to the moors, which I had only previously heard of. The houses were high and imposing. They were the closest I could imagine to palaces.

I counted the numbers until I found the house. I climbed the steps leading to the front door and knocked. Then I rang the bell. Then I did both again. Eventually I heard a noise and the door opened. It was Mrs. Atkinson but it was a shock to see her other than in her smart office clothes. She was wearing a simple nondescript multi-coloured dress with an apron and flat shoes. Her hair was down and just tied back on her neck.

"Oh yes, John. Come in. Mrs. Atkinson is not very well."

It was a shock to me at first to realise she shared the same name as her mother-in-law. She led me into the kitchen.

"Just sit there. I am taking some soup up for Mrs. Atkinson. While you are waiting you can take the string off that parcel. You will find some scissors in the drawer."

As part of my job I took great pride in tying and untying string without needing to cut it. Mr. Wilkinson had taught me about the arch sin known as 'waste'. I quickly got the string off but did not dare look inside the box.

Mrs. Atkinson reappeared with her tray.

"No, she won't look at it. Have you had your lunch John?" she asked.

"No," I said. "I left my sandwiches at work, Mrs. Atkinson."

"Good. You can eat this. I will cut you some bread and you can butter it yourself while I am trying on the new coat."

While she was cutting the bread she asked about my mother and my brothers and sister. Then she swept off with the parcel and a glint of excitement in her eye.

Whilst eating my soup, which tasted like no soup I had previously eaten, I had a chance to look around. The kitchen was very grand and seemed as big as the whole of our downstairs. There was a big range for cooking and baking, and several big dressers. There was other equipment which I did not know the purpose of. Off to the side was another door but it did not look like an outside door.

Just as I was finishing my soup, Mrs. Atkinson came to the kitchen door. Her appearance was closer to the normal lady I knew. Her hair was up on her head and she had shoes on with moderately high heels. The dominant feature was the magnificent red raincoat with big shoulders, a tight waist and an enormous skirt.

"Can you come and help me John," she said and led me into the hall.

There was a big mirror there and she had a small hand mirror which she gave to me.

"I am trying to see if the seams at the back are lying evenly and if the folds are hanging right. You hold the mirror up where I can see the back when I swirl the skirt."

She put her hands in the pockets and moved the skirt of the coat while I held the mirror. The trouble was, what I could see in the mirror was not what she could see. Her movements and my movements quickly became a compound error.

After several adjustments of position of me and the mirror, she was clearly becoming frustrated and annoyed.

"I know," she said impetuously, "you wear the coat and we won't need any mirrors."

She stopped and we both silently examined her suggestion. I was alarmed, incredulous and hoping my ears had not deceived me.

I realised she was serious when she started to undo the buttons of her coat.

"Come on," she said. "Take off that jacket! We can't have it making lumps under the smooth line of this coat. Better take your shirt off as well."

I may have blushed at this stage but any protest was no more than soundlessly opening and shutting my mouth.

She made encouraging noises as she helped me into the smooth sleeves and pulled the cool fabric over my bare arms and shoulders. It felt so good I thought I was going to faint. I stood there rigidly, as if I had been transformed into a pillar.

She buttoned the coat from the neck down but when she reached the waist, she stopped.

"No, those lumpy trousers will spoil the line. Better take them off."

At that point I certainly did blush and protested mildly.

"Oh don't be silly," she said, "with that coat on you won't be revealing anything. Now sit down over there, on the stairs, and take off your boots and trousers."

I did as I was told. Then I came back into the middle of the hall and stood in front of the mirror. What I saw, apart from the raincoat, did not impress me. However I felt I was wrapped in heaven. I could feel the smooth, cool, caressing rubber against my arms, my shoulders and my legs.

"Not a bad figure!" said Mrs. Atkinson with a fleeting smile. "Now put your hands in the pockets and twist your hips to swish the skirt like I was doing."

It did not come naturally. At one point she said, "Those woolen socks don't help. What size are your feet?"

I told her and she kicked off her shoes.

"Back on the stairs and take off those socks. Then try these shoes."

I realised then that we were remarkably similar in build. We were the same height in stocking feet. She had a slim figure for a woman and I had an emaciated one for a young man but they worked out about the same. Then to cap it all we had the same size feet.

It was the shoes that did it. Now I felt feminine. I could thrust my hips forward and rotate the hips. The skirt of the coat swished noisily and gloriously around my legs!

"Very good," said Mrs. Atkinson as she walked around me. I couldn't tell if she was referring to the way I moved or the coat moved. I did not care as I was in seventh heaven as all that delicious fabric swished and slithered around me.

"Now stand still," she said.

I could feel her fingers adjusting the folds and her

hands smoothing them down over my bottom. The feel of her hands on me made me tingle. I was not used to being touched in a gentle way, especially by a beautiful woman, and especially with my senses heightened by wearing this wonderful coat. I was totally unprepared for the combined effect all these things had on me.

"Now twist your hips again," she said.

I could hear her making approving noises but then we heard Mrs. Atkinson Senior coughing.

"I must go and see how she is," said Mrs. Atkinson. "Back in a minute," she called over her shoulder as she went up the stairs.

As soon as I was alone I had an opportunity to look at myself in the mirror. The body and feet looked fine both straight on and in profile. However, the feminine appearance was much reduced by my short hair.

I pulled my fringe down on to my forehead and pulled up the raincoat collar, as I had seen Mrs. Atkinson do. Now at least in profile, with only my nose, eyes and forehead visible, the general appearance was quite feminine.

I started to walk up and down the hall as if it was a catwalk, as I had seen the models do in the cinema newsreel. As I arrived at the mirror, I turned sharply, thrust my shoulders forward and raised my head archly, as I had also seen the models do. Meanwhile the coat swirled around my hips. I was really enjoying the feeling of what I would now call 'flamboyance'.

Then something made me stop! I turned slowly and looked up the stairs. There was Mrs. A sitting on the top stair, with her elbows resting on her knees and her chin in her hands. I had no idea how long she had been watching me.

"Well, well, well," she said slowly, with wry amusement.

5

The Secret

I had several weeks of work as normal to think over the wonderful events of that memorable visit to the Atkinson home. Mrs. Atkinson had not extended my visit on that day. She had come quickly downstairs and done a brief inspection of the back of the raincoat.

Then she had told me to take off the coat, put it over the banister knob and get dressed while she wrote a note for Mr. Wilkinson. Before I knew it I was back at the bus stop clutching my box and with my head reeling. It had been like a wonderful dream. I began to wonder when I would wake up.

Fortunately I had kept my bus tickets to give to Mr. Wilkinson with my change for the petty cash box.

I was pleased to see that my pile of boxes had not been fully used up. I was able to hide behind them and try to collect my thoughts. I realised with amazement that I was close to tears. I had no idea how that could be. I had not cried for years and associated it with pain or fear. So I just managed to look as if I was busy and tried not to think about anything. I didn't want to spoil the delicious feelings that were still coursing through my body.

I decided to walk home so I would have more time to think. I certainly wasn't going to tell my mother but what if Mrs. Atkinson told her? What if my mother asked me about it? What would I say? I was sure I would blush and give the game away.

For several days I was on tenterhooks waiting for my mother to ask me about my visit to Mrs. Atkinson's house.

But no questions came. I was too young and innocent to realise that Mrs. Atkinson would not have come out well from telling anyone about what happened either. Gradually the incident subsided to being a happy secret memory.

Then a few weeks later Mr. Wilkinson called me into his office at about the same time.

"Get ahead with your boxes John. Mrs. Atkinson wants you to take some papers up to the house so she can check them. You are to wait and bring them back."

I was pleased at the prospect of an outing but knew there would be no raincoat to try on this time. However the prospect of seeing Mrs. Atkinson on her own again was appealing. I hadn't seen her going to or from the office lately.

This time I remembered my sandwiches. I even made the effort to comb my hair before I left. I felt I needed to make a good impression. I felt there was some sort of test coming.

When I arrived I observed that Mrs. Atkinson was looking a lot smarter than the last time I visited. She was wearing what I would call a smart grey dress and medium-heeled black shoes. She was wearing some lipstick and jewellery. Her hair was up on top of her head and I thought she was the most sophisticated-looking lady I could imagine. I am not sure I even knew the word 'sophisticated' then but she certainly fulfilled my ideal image of a glamorous, stylish lady.

She invited me into the kitchen again and asked me to sit at the big wooden table in the middle of the room.

"Have you got your sandwiches this time?" she asked kindly.

I said I had and she offered me a cup of tea. I had been working in a warehouse long enough to know there was no limit to the cups of tea one could drink.

While I was eating my sandwiches, Mrs. Atkinson sat

down at the table and pulled the folder I had brought towards her.

"When you have finished your sandwiches John, I want you to help me with some figures.

"This folder is full of orders taken by one of our representatives. I need to reconcile these with his claims for commission and travelling expenses."

I was apprehensive. This sounded like a lot of responsibility. It sounded like what I was being asked to do was going to get someone into trouble with the firm or, even worse, with the police.

"Don't look worried John. The figures will tell whether my suspicions are true or false. Do you know what a ready-reckoner is?"

She explained that it was a book of listed calculations and showed me how to find the answer to each calculation based on the figures she gave me.

She called out. "Blackberry Mayfair at £4 19 shillings and 11 pence," and the quantity ordered. I would look up the page with that price and quantity and tell her the answer. She would write it down in a list. This laborious process was the way things were done before the arrival of office calculators.

At the end of each page she would give me the sheet and ask me to total the figures in my head and write the answer in pencil at the bottom. Then she would check the sheet herself.

I was lucky that mental arithmetic was one of the things I'd been good at school. However I found it boring totaling columns just for the sake of it. Doing this had some purpose. In addition, I thought each time of the delicious raincoats that each sum represented.

Periodically we were interrupted by noises from upstairs and Glynis would go up to see the condition of Mrs. Atkinson Senior. By about 4 o'clock I was beginning to fade.

Glynis however was hot on the trail.

"Now let us reconcile these figures to the actual claims," she said.

She pulled out another sheet of paper that had weekly totals. We checked one against the other and found the differences she had suspected.

"Right John, I think I have everything I need," she said with a wicked smile on her face. She piled the papers on top of each other and put them back in the folder.

"Would you like another cup of tea? There is something I want to talk to you about."

I accepted but with mixed feelings. Was she going to raise the subject of me showing too much enthusiasm about wearing the raincoat? Was she going to tell my mother?

It wasn't about that at all. She explained that she was now limited to the times she could come down to the factory because of the failing health of Mrs. Atkinson Senior.

She had a cleaning lady who had worked for Mrs. Atkinson Senior for years. She came in for a couple of days regularly, even though there wasn't that much cleaning to do. She would also come for some extra hours by arrangement. However Glynis explained that did not give her enough time to do everything she needed to do at the office.

She had decided to set up an office at home so she could work there the rest of the week. However she was finding it difficult having the right things and information in the right place. Also some of the figures she needed only became available at certain times of the week when she wasn't there.

"What I need, John, is an assistant who could become a kind of secretary. They would have to bring things from the factory and find particular information as I need it. Also, they would have to carry out some instructions for me back at the factory. How does that sound to you, John?"

She carried on without letting me answer.

"Both Mr. Wilkinson and your mother say you are bright and willing. Your assistance this afternoon showed me you can handle figures. What do you say, John?"

I was somewhat overwhelmed by the variety of thoughts and questions. I was also once again annoyed that people had been talking about me. All I could manage to say was that I thought secretaries were usually girls.

"Not at all John!"

She told me that for many years political figures and industrialists had had secretaries who were men. It was only with the increase in use of the typewriter that women became predominant.

"And…I suppose during the recent wars," she continued, "there were fewer men available to do that sort of work.

"In fact in the old days it was a sort of apprenticeship. How else did people learn the skills of handling such responsibility

"Mind you John, there is something else I must tell you. They were usually called 'Confidential Secretaries'. Do you know why John?"

"Was it because they were expected not to talk about what they saw and heard when helping this important person?"

"Excellent John! This arrangement can only work if you are completely silent about anything you get to know as a result of helping me. Your mother and Mr. Wilkinson say you keep yourself to yourself. Maybe you are a bit secretive? Can I count on you to be discreet?"

She now stopped and waited until I answered.

"Yes, Mrs. Atkinson."

"Good, well both of us will have to keep our secrets then," she said slowly and ominously.

"Now run along. You can go straight home now. I will telephone Mr. Wilkinson to tell him you have gone home. I will have to talk to Mr. Wilkinson tomorrow about arrangements and I know he will be sorry to lose you. So your discretion includes not saying anything to him until he tells you. Is that clear?"

It wasn't until I was on the bus that I realised two things. One was that Mrs. Atkinson had not really given me a choice about taking this new job. As I was to learn, there was no gainsaying Mrs. Atkinson. By a mixture of authority, personality and charm, Mrs. Atkinson nearly always got her way.

The second was the remark about both of us keeping secrets. Could it be that she was not above a little blackmail to ensure she got the discretion she considered so important?

6

The Confession

For a week or two after the meeting I carried on just as before while Mrs. Atkinson was in close negotiations with Mr. Wilkinson. He was not going to be able to find another lad to do my job that quickly.

However even before a replacement was found, the pattern of my work started to change. In the morning I would build up my stack of boxes and in the afternoon I would go and help in the accounts department. They would collect data from the various departments of the company. The people who did this were very set in their ways. They had worked for the department for many years and were all very suspicious of me. I later realised they were also pretty suspicious of each other.

They would all do their data collecting and provide their weekly reports to Mrs. Atkinson but didn't have any idea how it all fitted together. Only Mrs. Atkinson could do that in order to know whether the firm was working efficiently or not. With the information she got on a weekly basis she could mount investigations into the various departments to find out why certain things weren't happening, fabric was being lost or money was being wasted.

She explained I didn't need to be able to do the jobs of these people but to know what their job consisted of and what data could be obtained from each section of the accounts department. She clearly wanted me as her information collecting machine, who would bring her all the data for her to interpret. I realised later that her training in the fashion ateliers of Paris before the war taught her the power of highly centralised administrative control. I also realised why there was such high importance given to discretion. I was the only other person who would possibly be able to interpret the data to know what was going on.

She found me quick to understand the internal workings of the company and after a few weeks suggested I went to evening classes to learn about book-keeping and other parts of the accounting process. This was very interesting because I could relate what I was learning to what I was doing on a daily basis.

I was really enjoying my role and rarely thought that underlying all the statistics I was processing were beautiful rubberised raincoats that gave glamour to so many ladies around the country. I didn't even see Mrs. Atkinson wearing any of her raincoats because I only ever saw her at her house or occasionally at the office. I didn't mind too much because now my other interest, getting on in the world, was coming about.

Periodically my mother would say she was continuing to get good reports from Mrs. Atkinson and I should make sure I did exactly as I was told. This brought up the usual feelings of resentment about being talked about behind my back. However I knew better than to say anything to my mother.

On one occasion my mother said we had a lot to be grateful for from Atkinson's and in particular from Glynis Atkinson. She wouldn't elaborate but it was at that point I first guessed that she was probably receiving financial help with the house and family directly from Mrs. Atkinson. My own pay had gone up but not by much and my mother had not asked me for more. She had encouraged me to spend the money on better clothes for work and on books.

My new routine was that I would go into the office first thing in the morning and do my data collection work. I would wait until about 11 o'clock to see if there were any requests for additional information that Mrs. Atkinson wanted me to take. Then I would go up to the house with my new shiny briefcase full of the information I had collected.

Mrs. Atkinson would prepare lunch for us both and we would talk about all sorts of things before we got down to interpreting the information I had brought.

One day at the end of lunch. Mrs. Atkinson put down her cutlery and cleared her throat.

"John, there is something I want to talk to you about." she said slowly.

I had an ominous feeling that the long-awaited and dreaded moment had come.

"Do you mind me asking you about the time you wore the red raincoat for me in the hall here?"

I knew Glynis Atkinson well enough to know that although it was a polite question, there was only one answer. We were going to talk about it!

"Can you tell me about it?" she said in a matter of fact way.

I thought of trying to deny it or pretend I didn't remember but I knew my vivid blush had already betrayed me. The best I could do was shake my head and gasp for breath.

I felt waves of panic. I knew she had seen what I had done but it remained at a distance as long it was not spoken about. Now she wanted to talk about it. Worse still she wanted me to talk about it.

I thought of running away but that would not have solved anything. Deep down I knew this dragon would have to be faced.

The best I could do was gasp. "I can't talk about it'. I was surprised to hear my own voice come out sounding so unreal.

"Just sit there a minute," she said gently and moved to get up.

More panic - what was she going to do? She moved to the sink and poured a glass of water. I was very glad of it because I was beginning to feel sick. Fortunately I wasn't chewing food at the time or I may have vomited.

She came and sat close to me while I sipped the water and struggled to stop the heaving in my chest. For a long time she said nothing.

"John, you know me well enough to know the two things I prize more highly than any other." I said nothing.

"Honesty and discretion, John, are the two most important ingredients of what we might call character." She paused.

"I have not told anybody about that day, nor do I intend to." She paused again.

"I realise it may be very difficult for you to talk about it but I have my reasons for asking. I may be able to tell you about them in due course. Do you trust me to keep my word about not telling anyone else?"

"Yes," I managed to blurt out with some emotion.

"Well, let's try again shall we?"

At first I tried to diminish it by shaking my head but I could see the disappointment in her brown eyes, though she didn't say anything.

As I got my voice back I started to go back to my childhood interest in the clothes that women wore. Not so much the clothes worn by working women like my mother and grandmother but by younger women. I was particularly drawn to more sensuous fabrics and the way they moved and even the noise they made. Most attractive of all were the rubberised raincoats that many better dressed women wore.

I even admitted that I had on occasion even followed a lady wearing such a coat just to watch the way the fabric moved as her hips swung.

I told her that when I had a chance, I would look through women's magazines for illustrations of glamorous clothes and in particular for raincoats and could not believe my luck when my mother got me a job at Atkinson's. Also of my disappointment at not having any contact with the lovely coats that Atkinson's made.

As I grew more confident I felt able to tell her how much I admired how she looked in the coats that she wore. I even told her how impressed I was by her appearance on the day I first met her.

I had been talking while looking down at the table. I was drawing out patterns with my finger. Suddenly I realised that I had been weeping. I don't know when it started but I suppose it was the bottled-up emotion seeping out.

When I had finished I looked up. I must have caught her unexpectedly because she had her handkerchief out and was wiping away a tear. I looked down again very quickly.

For a while there was silence. Then she spoke.

"Thank you for telling me John," she said softly. "So when I asked you to try on the sample coat here, was that the first time you had ever felt the fabric against your skin?"

"Yes it was, but it was just how I imagined it."

"And how was that?"

"It felt soft and cool as it lay on my arms and brushed against my legs. It made me feel safe and secure, and also strong."

I didn't tell her it made me feel feminine and that made me feel sexually excited. Somehow she knew I had held something back. She made an expectant sound as if knowing there was more.

Back came the blushes and the tears as I stumbled out with the words laced with acute embarrassment.

"But what is the matter with that?" she asked.

"I am supposed to be a boy who wants to be a man. How can I be a man if I have feelings like that?"

"Unfortunately real life is not always as tidy as we are led to believe," she said comfortingly. After a pause she added in a slightly husky voice, "That is enough for today John. We can talk about this again another time, if you want to."

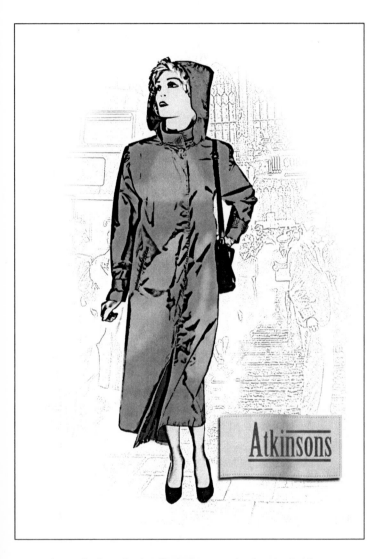

A set of enlarged colour illustrations may be downloaded from
www.dominantdesigns.co.uk or
email: **pictures@dominantdesigns.co.uk**

7

The Competitor

One morning I was in the office collating the figures to take to Mrs. Atkinson. I heard an unmistakable step on the stairs. I knew from long experience when Mr. Wilkinson was coming and that I had to look busy. Out of habit I got my head down into the figures I was working on just as he came into the office.

"John, I have got something for you to take to Mrs. Atkinson."

Out of respect for my previous boss who had been so good to me and for me, I stood up.

"My goodness you've grown up," he said. I didn't know what he meant at first and now realised that I was nearly as tall as him.

"Still could do with putting a bit more meat on you," he said in a fatherly way.

Looking back now we can see that the war and post-war rationing had left its mark on us growing youngsters. Although I was now in my mid-teens, I was physically some years behind.

There was never any danger of starving; my mother would have done whatever it took to make sure we had enough not to be hungry. And you could always fill a gap with good old bread and dripping. But in those days extra money, even if you had it, couldn't buy more or better food, at least not if you came from our kind of background. We had all heard of the Black Market and Spivs who could get you anything. However we had never come across any so we had to manage with what our meagre ration books could provide.

There was no danger of the diseases of malnutrition because as children we got free orange juice and cod liver oil. However, that did not provide muscle and bone-building protein that a growing adolescent requires. I was painfully thin and most conspicuous of all was that my voice had not broken.

"Mrs. Atkinson has asked me to give you this to take up to the house." He was carrying one of the familiar boxes from the warehouse, well and truly tied with string.

"What is it?" I asked impetuously.

"I am sure Mrs. Atkinson will tell you, if she wants you to know," said Mr. Wilkinson stuffily. "Now I have got work to do. Your replacement is not as reliable as you were. Can't leave him alone for long!"

Despite his kindly parting words, I had been put in my place by a touch of what I had come to think of as the Atkinson's disease. The main symptom of this condition was that everybody thought the little they knew about what was going on was a great secret. They thought it gave them a bit of status to know something that other people did not know.

"I will make sure she gets it," I said distantly as I took the box. I noted that it was about the weight of a single raincoat. Something she wants to inspect, I thought, possibly a return from a retail customer.

I had to hunch up against the weather as I waited at the bus stop. It was one those classic Brunley days where everything was wet and squelchy. Fortunately I did not have to wait long for my bus up the hill.

When I arrived Glynis was clearly not in a good mood. As she opened the door she said: "Is that the box from Mr. Wilkinson?" Then seeing how wet I was she told me to come in out of the wet in a much more considerate tone.

Once inside she took the box and hurried to the

kitchen table. She got out a pair of scissors and was just about to hack off the string.

"Let me please," I said, stepping quickly up to the box. Fortunately Mr. Wilkinson's training in his knot work meant I could undo it very quickly and Glynis's impatience did not have time to boil over.

"May I open it?" I said.

"No! I'll do it," she said as she grabbed at the string.

Inside, not surprisingly, was a raincoat. It was a light purple colour. I suppose one could call it lilac. The most noticeable thing about it was the texture of the outside. It had a crispy texture and glistened like nothing I had seen before.

"What is it Mrs. Atkinson?" I asked.

"It is crepe. It is much lighter than the cotton we use. It has a surface texture that is much finer than cotton but I don't believe it can do the job."

She held the coat up in front of her and examined the seams. "The taping seems to be holding but I can't believe it can be waterproof."

Then she had a thought. "There is only one way to find out. Let's test it."

She turned to me. "Take off your jacket and put on the raincoat John."

She said it without a flicker of recognition or relation to our previous conversations.

Slowly and carefully I lifted the coat over my shoulders and slid my arms into the sleeves. It was like walking into a welcoming waterfall. I was so overcome by the exhilaration of the experience I fumbled with the buttons. This was partly because they were the wrong way round to what I was used to. Glynis moved in and did the buttons for me, sealing me into the delicious coat.

"Now turn around and let me see how the seams are placed," she said.

I could feel her fingers following the lines from my shoulders down to the waist.

Next she fastened the belt around my waist.

"It is a bit lumpy down there with your pullover and trousers but it will have to do for the moment."

Then she pulled up the hood and tied the two strings under my chin with a double knot. She pulled the sides of the hood forward so I felt like a horse wearing blinkers. I could only see straight in front. To either side all I could see was the lilac rubberised fabric. If I turned my head slightly I could feel its softness on my cheek.

"Right, follow me."

She led me from the kitchen through the other door, into a sort of washroom and then to an outside door which she unlocked and opened. She stood back and said. "Go out and get this supposed raincoat wet and we shall see."

Mrs. Atkinson had a very dismissive attitude to all raincoats that were not made by Atkinson's. She referred to the coat I was wearing with almost a sneer in her voice.

She put her hand in the middle of my back and pushed me gently through the door out onto the back step. Gingerly I stepped down onto the flagstone terrace and took a few steps. In front of me was a long garden falling away from the house. The end of the garden was barely visible in the mist and rain. I noticed that it was not raining as heavily as when I had arrived half an hour earlier.

I heard a creak behind me. I turned my head but all I saw was more lilac hood. To find the origin of the creak, I had to turn my whole body. I saw Glynis at the open kitchen window.

"Walk around," she said.

"Where?" I replied.

"Just walk up and down the terrace. Wiggle your hips like you did last time!" she said with a smile. With that she closed the window.

I could feel the patter of raindrops on my shoulders and on the hood. I felt I was trapped inside this lovely coat. I couldn't have taken it off, with its awkward buttons and knotted hood, even if I had wanted to. But I didn't want to. I enjoyed being a prisoner in this glorious lilac rubberised raincoat.

The rain was definitely diminishing but I found if I stood close to the house I would catch the drips falling from the gutter. I was looking down the garden when I heard a tapping behind me. Mrs. Atkinson had set up her office in the dining room where she was working on her papers. She was tapping on the window and signaling to keep moving up and down the terrace.

I tried to find interesting things to look through my restricted field of vision. The only consolation to my growing boredom was to think I was fulfilling my dream of wearing a woman's rubberised raincoat. I had put my hands in the pockets, which was my normal place to keep them when I wasn't doing anything. I found that the insides of the pockets were unlined so I could feel the smooth rubberised fabric against my hand.

When I turned my back briefly on the window, I could press my hands against my upper legs and into my groin but unfortunately I couldn't feel anything through my thick trousers.

Sometimes, as I turned at the end of the terrace, I had a quick look at my reflection in the window. Because the hood limited my side vision, I could only see myself from directly in front as I turned. I stopped for a few seconds. I could see my body from my waist upwards so I did not have to look below the hem line of the coat. To my eyes this upper part looked surprisingly feminine, just like one of those lovely ladies I used to stare at in the street in their rubberised raincoats. It gave me a very deep thrill of wonder to realise this was actually me.

Eventually I heard the kitchen window open. Before I could turn to face my hood towards the window, I heard Mrs. Atkinson say "You can come back into the washroom now."

As she let me in she said: "Stand on the tiles over there." I noticed there was actually water dripping off the coat onto the tiles. As she undid me from my encasement she passed me a towel. "You will need this," she said.

She turned the coat inside out and put it on a hanger which she hung from a drying rail which could be pulled up towards the ceiling on a rope. She was examining the fabric and seams for signs of water penetration.

Foolishly I asked what the towel was for. I knew very well what she had expected and now she was disappointed to find no signs of the raincoat having let in water.

"Shut up," was all she said. I think if I had been closer she might have hit me.

Then she came and looked at my shirt for signs of water.

"Maybe it wasn't raining heavily enough," she said but I could tell from her tone that she was not that convinced.

Then she gave a light laugh saying, "Maybe I should make us a cup of tea?"

As I was getting to know her better I realised that Glynis could switch very quickly from being seriously angry to laughing at herself. It was very endearing to see behind her serious work face, which was all they saw of her at Atkinson's.

When we had our cups of tea in front of us at the kitchen table, Mrs. Atkinson explained what the matter was. She had received disturbing reports from her representatives who called on the shops who were their customers. Some were saying that Atkinson's was not keeping up with the times. They said that customers wanted lighter and more feminine coats in more glamorous materials.

Atkinson's had always prided itself on the sturdiness of its garments. They used the best quality Manchester cotton to carry the rubber backing. They had been dyed in bright colours by the best dyers but with the added thickness of the rubber, the fabric was a little stiff. The result was a very serviceable raincoat but it could be seen as a bit heavy and utilitarian.

Now raincoats were coming in from abroad which used softer, lighter fabrics such as rubberised satin, crepe, taffeta and even silk. Mrs. Atkinson's immediate response was that they could not be weatherproof. She had asked several of her most trusted representatives to go to shops where they were not known, or send their wives, to purchase one of these new raincoats for her to inspect.

The first one had proved weatherproof, albeit not in the worst weather possible. Others were to follow. I was told that I would have to go through this operation again when the other coats arrived.

My reaction was one of anticipation but mixed with dislike of the boredom of just walking around on the terrace. I told Mrs. Atkinson that it could get rather boring.

She quickly overcame that problem by saying next time I could walk along the path which ran round the garden.

"Ten times round the garden should do," she said with a glint of mischievous satisfaction in her eye.

Then she thought for a while.

"You know John," she paused, "when you were walking around on the terrace there were times when you could almost have passed for a girl. We would have to do something about your trousers and boots. Those were a bit of a giveaway!" she laughed.

"Another thing that let you down," she continued,

"was your posture! Much of the time you slouched around with your shoulders hunched and your hands in the pockets of that very expensive coat. I half-expected to see you kick a pebble! If we are going to do anything with you John, you will have to learn how to walk properly!"

Since Mrs. Atkinson was not so much speaking to me but about me, I didn't feel I needed to say anything.

However my imagination was racing. "I wonder what she means by 'do anything with me'," I thought to myself. "Does she mean what I think she means?" More accurately it was. "Does she mean what I hope she means?"

My thoughts were cut short by her next words.

"Time to get back to work."

8

The First Lesson

Over the next week two other boxes were given to me by Mr. Wilkinson to take up to Mrs. Atkinson. I accepted them with an appearance of indifference which hid my feelings of excitement and anticipation.

The day I took the first of these boxes up to the house was a bright winter's day. It was bitterly cold even in the sunshine, and without a cloud in the sky.

Mrs. Atkinson examined the raincoat carefully and tried it on. She even made some approving noises. It was a delicate shade of green and looked very spring-like. As with all these continental coats the fabric had an extra crispness and swish. I thought one could call it apple green. It would be lovely to wear in spring or summer when the weather would be a mixture of sunshine and showers.

"There is little point in you wearing this coat outside today. However at lunchtime I want you to try on a few things which will improve your appearance when we have a suitable day."

I had difficulty concentrating on my figures that morning as I thought what Mrs. Atkinson could mean by 'a few things'.

Eventually lunchtime came and Mrs. Atkinson came into the kitchen where I worked. She was carrying some clothes over her arm. She looked troubled.

"Before we go any further John, I want to be sure that this is really what you want. I can dress you as a girl so you can wear raincoats and other clothes and look the part. But... I need to hear from you that is what you really want. I need to be sure it is not me putting something on you for my own reasons."

Unusually her voice trailed off as she considered her own thoughts. It was my turn to be troubled.

"I don't know what you mean Mrs. Atkinson," I said in some confusion.

She straightened up. "Never mind about that, are you sure you want me to dress you up?"

I realised that I would have to take a firm position as she was obviously having doubts.

"Yes please," I heard myself saying.

"Good," she said, clearly taking back control. "Here are your new clothes. If you are going to look feminine you will need to feel feminine, so I have picked out a few of my older things which can now become yours."

She showed me a pair of knickers made in some thin, smooth fabric with thin elastic around the waist and legs. Then there was a roll-on girdle from which hung four suspenders.

Next she showed me a slip which was noticeably narrower around the knees than at the waist. It was made of a much thicker material than the knickers but about the same colour. She called this a 'deportment slip'. She said its purpose was to teach young girls how to walk in a feminine way. Because it restricted you around the knees, you could only take small steps. She explained it was much more feminine to take two small steps than one stride. It also meant when you sat down you did not let your knees come apart in the way men did.

"Next comes the brassiere! I don't know if you have seen one of these before," she said holding up a white brassiere.

"When you have got everything else on I will help you with this. Now go into the downstairs toilet and get changed. If you need any help come back in here, don't make a noise that might wake Mrs. Atkinson, who is having her afternoon sleep."

All I was able to do was to put on the knickers. The girdle went up around my waist in a bunch but I didn't know how to unroll it either up or down. I realised that there was no point in trying to put on the stockings unless the suspenders were available to attach to them.

After a few minutes struggling with the girdle, I realised how cold it was in the toilet so I scooped up everything and went back into the kitchen. As I knocked and came in Glynis could clearly see I was in some confusion.

"Go and stand by the fire and I will help you in a minute," she said slightly impatiently.

"I suppose it must be difficult if you have no experience of these things," she said in a more kindly tone. She showed me how to smooth the girdle over my tummy and bottom, although there wasn't much of either. Then she made me sit down and showed me how to put on stockings without laddering them.

"Now put on the slip before you put on any shoes," she said. I immediately felt what she meant about restriction as I had to keep my knees together in a way that was quite unfamiliar.

She went to the cloakroom and came back with a pair of low-heeled shoes. "These will do for the moment, wearing high heels takes quite a bit of getting used to."

Next we did the bra. It fitted surprisingly well but Mrs. Atkinson had to find some dusters to make into balls to fill the two cups.

Then she stood back to review her handiwork.

"Not bad," she said, "but you are still shivering; you had better put your shirt back on. No, I have a better idea. Just wait a minute."

She left the room and returned a few minutes later with a coat over her arm.

"Put this on," she said passing me the coat. I realised

by its weight and feel that it was rubber-lined. Although I was cold, that did not inhibit me from putting it on and experiencing a delicious shiver as my skin encountered it.

"You will soon warm it up and this food will help too," said Mrs. A., who was now back at the stove pouring out our soup.

I sat in my place swathed in the lovely feeling of this coat with a steaming bowl of delicious soup in front of me and several pieces of bread and butter.

'Life can't get much better than this!' I thought to myself.

As we were eating Mrs. Atkinson asked me if I recognised the coat I was wearing. It was a medium grey colour, long and full at the hem. It had a hood but I thought it might be too difficult to eat with the hood up.

"I will give you a clue. It used to be silver!"

I was stunned.

"Yes, it was the one you said I was wearing the first time you met me. It was a sample made in a new fabric we were trying. That is the trouble with innovating. You find out that things are not as good as they should be. The silver did not last and now you see it has become an anonymous grey. Fortunately we hadn't gone into full production when it started to lose its shine. We sent the fabric back to the manufacturer, but I kept the coat. It can be yours to wear when you are here, if you like!"

All I could do was blink with pleasure and gratitude and eventually get out the words. "Thank you, Mrs. Atkinson."

After lunch I had my first deportment lesson. There was only room to take a couple of steps in the kitchen, which was just as well because I could easily have fallen over in my unfamiliar shoes and very tight underskirt.

Glynis had trained as a model before the war and she showed me first how to stand. The girdle held my stomach in and reminded me to keep my waist upright. My big problem was, as Glynis said, my shoulders.

"It comes from too many years shambling around with your hands in your pockets. It causes your shoulders to hunch forward and you inevitably bend your spine forward."

She arranged me, showing me how to push my hips forward and balance my upper body so my newly acquired bosom was presented. Most important was the way one held one's head so that one had what she called "hauteur'. I didn't know the intricacies then but when I got the position she wanted, it felt wonderfully feminine but also strong.

"There is something wrong," she said. "It's that dreadful hairstyle. Your hair is quite long for a boy but it has no shape to it. Just a minute!"

Off she went again and this time returned with a hat. It was a sort of turban which fitted close to the head and covered all my hair.

"That's better; you look quite feminine now, even without any make-up."

She showed me how to move on the spot and strike another pose, as if for a photograph. Somehow I seemed to get it very quickly.

"Good, that shows great promise," she said. "Next time we will clear some space in the dining room so you can have a decent space to walk. I want to see a different posture next time you walk on the terrace."

"That is enough for today, it is time to get back to work. Get dressed and leave your new clothes at the bottom of the stairs. But remember, I want you to practice walking better in normal life with your shoulders erect. Pretend to yourself that you are wearing your heels as you walk. And when you are sure nobody is looking, thrust out your hips and chest in the way I have shown you. Above all keep your hands out of your pockets."

All my life I had been followed by the cry *'Take your*

hands out of your pockets'. My mother had said it, my teachers had said it and Mr. Wilkinson had said it. Now Mrs. Atkinson had given me a reason to do it, I was determined that from now on I would.

A set of enlarged colour illustrations may be downloaded from
www.dominantdesigns.co.uk or
email: **pictures@dominantdesigns.co.uk**

9

Mrs. Atkinson Explains

Every day now I was busy with my accounting work and record-keeping for Mrs. Atkinson. While I was at the office I would compile all the production records onto a weekly summary. I would also compile all the sales records that came from the sales representatives and from direct orders to a weekly sales summary. I would then reconcile the dispatch department records to see which orders had been fulfilled and which were still waiting. I also had periodic stock records of fabric and buying records to reconcile.

I took this information up to the house for Mrs. A to scrutinise. She would then telephone the various departments to find out why certain things weren't being done. I also had to enter the summary information into big record books.

At the time I didn't realise it but Mrs. A must have been one of the first practitioners of 'scientific management' that became the business norm in the 1950s and 1960s. But then neither did she! She evolved this system, with me as its eyes, ears and legs, because of the situation she found herself in.

Once Mrs. Atkinson Senior took to her bed, that meant she needed someone with her nearly all the time. Glynis accepted that as her responsibility. She had Mrs. Holroyd, who had been their cleaner for years beyond reckoning, and who came in for a couple of days each week.

The house didn't need that much cleaning these days but Glynis was happy to pay Mrs. Holroyd to sit with Mrs. Atkinson and make cups of tea for her. Doctor Renshaw would pop in on most mornings at the end of his rounds just to see how old Mrs Atkinson was doing. He had said there was nothing that could be done for her except to keep her comfortable while she slowly declined.

So Glynis had evolved a distance management system so that she knew what was going on at the factory without being there every day. She had devised the forms I had to complete and periodically refined them to give her more useful information. Also, because of her 'divide and rule' style, she could be sure that the departments would report to her any difficulties they had with any other departments.

I was used as her unofficial eyes and ears to find out how much truth there was in the reports she received. I learned a lot about human nature while doing this.

At first I was not trusted because of my youth and because I did not have any official authority. I would take an oblique approach by saying "Mrs. Atkinson has asked me to ask you if you can clarify this situation..."

Once an unsatisfactory situation had been exposed, I asked or even suggested how it could be handled so that I could tell Mrs. Atkinson that it had been spotted and was already being put right. This meant that they thought Mrs. A would think that the solution or improvement was their idea.

Of course she knew it was my idea or hers because she had suggested how it could be addressed. This way dignity and appearances of competence could be maintained. This sort of management without authority was a very useful skill to learn and it stood me in very good stead in later life.

On a number of occasions I had deep conversations with Mrs. Atkinson. Actually they were more like monologues but I relaised later that she just needed someone to talk to. These conversations showed me that although she thought a lot about what she was doing, her confidence in herself was not as great as she portrayed.

On one occasion she was a bit depressed and allowed herself to show it with me.

"I am not a business woman," she said. "I find myself running this business because my father-in-law died during the war and my husband was too busy with war work to run it, as it was expected he would.

"Then my husband died and I am left to run the business on my own with an ailing mother-in-law to support. She is now bed-ridden and needs constant attention. I should have just quit and gone back to France after the war but … I felt it was my duty to stay.

"Now I have to put on this facade of being a competent business woman but what training or experience do I have? All I know is a little bit about fashion and pattern making."

She was doing herself a great injustice of course. She was a shrewd business woman and had learnt how to manage and manipulate people during her fashion career before the war in Paris. However I had come to realise that Mrs. A was lonely and felt trapped in her situation.

Once she had got into running a peace-time business she realised she had flair because she had a unique sympathy with her customers.

She also learned the very special features of the fabric and clothing that she worked with. She explained it to me once.

"What people don't realise is that rubber is a natural substance. It harmonises with our bodies in a way that synthetic things cannot. That is why we use only natural rubber.

"When a lady wears one of our raincoats she should not wear heavy clothes underneath. If she wears just a thin layer underneath, the rubber can harmonise with her body temperature to keep her warm and comfortable, as well as dry. If she wears heavy clothes her body will overheat and the excess heat cannot escape. It is very nice to feel rain hitting your coat but knowing that it is not getting you wet or making you cold. A well-sealed raincoat will also protect a lady very well from a sharp cold wind.

"Then there is the physical sensation of feeling the rubber against your skin or through a thin blouse. For some women this is an intensely sensuous experience and it gives them great pleasure and comfort.

"How do I know this?" you might ask.

"Well I have quite a few customers who write to me and tell me how much they appreciate our raincoats and they tell me how it feels to wear them.

"I try to reply personally to them all. Do you know why that is, John?"

"No," I said. Mrs. A had a very serious air about her.

"Well the war has left a lot of disappointed women. Some of them are widows, but there are many others whose lives were devastated by the war. Sometimes it was what they had to go through with bombing, deprivation, evacuation, and worry. These things leave scars.

"Then there were the things their husbands experienced. Many came home scarred mentally. Their wives find themselves living with strangers, not the person they originally married. They keep up appearances but many of those men are mental wrecks whose main preoccupation is just staying sane. They have little to give in the way of consideration or love.

"It might seem trivial to other people but for many women the caresses their skin gets from their raincoat are all they get.

"Has it ever occurred to you why most raincoats are sold unlined?"

Before I could answer she continued.

"We have tried offering our raincoats with soft fabric linings but they don't sell. It seems like our customers really want to experience the sensual feeling of the rubber against their skin and through their clothing.

"Then we have customers who tell me they enjoy the smell of the rubber when it gets warm against their skin. Many say their raincoat makes them feel more feminine than any of their other clothes. They say that the combination of the feel of the fabric, the way it moves and the rustling noise it makes, all combine to make them feel beautiful, attractive and stronger.

"In the old days, those who had the opportunity to go to balls and dances could wear extravagant dresses that made them feel feminine and attractive. In these days of austerity, very few ladies can do that and with passing years they don't have the confidence in their good looks any more.

"Their big glamorous raincoat has the sound and feel of a glamorous evening dress and can be worn nearly every day in this climate. There is little doubt that our raincoats, worn well, do get admiration from both men and women.

"There are even some who go out wearing their coats well fastened but underneath they have only their underwear. They say it excites them to be the only one who knows how little they are wearing underneath. They admit that it adds a stimulant to their sexuality and it makes them feel quite naughty.

"I have even had customers who say when they feel lonely, vulnerable or insecure they will go to bed wearing their raincoat. They say it gives them comfort and strength. So you see John," she said smiling at me, "you are far from being alone in your desire to experience the pleasure and consolation of close contact with this wonderful substance."

On another occasion I asked Mrs. Atkinson why most of our raincoats had hoods. Ladies could use an umbrella instead to keep their head and hair dry.

"I take a pride in knowing our customers, John," she said.

"Our main customer is Mrs. Housewife who has to go on the bus to and from the shops. When she gets off the bus she may have to walk half a mile carrying a couple of shopping bags and a handbag. Maybe she has a pram or a pushchair to manage as well, or a young child on reins. She doesn't have a hand available for an umbrella. She needs both hands.

"Imagine waiting at an open bus stop in the rain on a windy day with a young child. Wouldn't you be glad of the protection of a securely fastened hood?"

I often thought about those conversations. The depths of Mrs. A's knowledge of people and humanity impressed me. As I learned more about her and her life, I realised she had received her education in a very hard school.

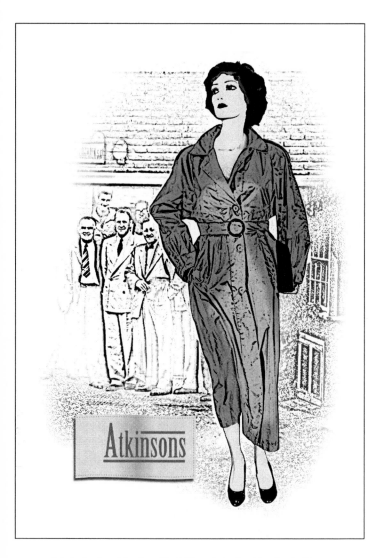

A set of enlarged colour illustrations may be downloaded from
www.dominantdesigns.co.uk   or
email: **pictures@dominantdesigns.co.uk**

10

A Testing Time

Needless to say the other competitive raincoats also proved to be waterproof, despite their apparent flimsiness. After the initial tests in her garden, Mrs. Atkinson seemed to develop a taste for this sort of real-life experimentation.

It started a few weeks later when she told me that she was being asked to change the glue used for taping the seams of Atkinson's raincoats. Getting the old natural glue product from abroad was proving difficult. So she was persuaded to try some new synthetic substitutes. She was as ever cautious about changing from what was working satisfactorily. She said she would have some samples made with the alternative glues.

"You will have to test them John. I'm sure you won't mind will you?" she said with an amused glint in her eye.

One of the things Mrs. A. rarely did was to really ask. She assumed your agreement with whatever she wanted. If you didn't want to do something, you had to lodge an objection. This was not something you would do lightly. In fairness to Mrs. A, she would often accept my objections, if they were based on logical reasoning. However I guessed that the sycophants down at the factory would rather bite their tongues off than argue with Mrs. Atkinson.

We had established a vastly improved routine for testing raincoats since the first days of my walking listlessly back and forth on the terrace. Mrs. A told me she had been planning to have some work done in the back garden and now she had an additional reason to do so.

She had some more steps made leading down into

the garden. This meant there were steps at either end of the terrace. At the bottom of the steps she had a gravel path laid which ran around the garden and then back to the bottom of the other steps. So this meant there was now a circuit. It started from the top of the steps near the back door, down the steps, around the path, back up the other steps and then across the terrace back to the beginning.

At least I wouldn't get my feet sopping wet walking on the grass as I had to do in the early forays into the garden. We had resolved that by my wearing Mrs. A's gardening Wellingtons but that didn't do much for my feelings of femininity. It also didn't do much for my feminine appearance or feminine posture.

Then Mrs. Atkinson told me she was planning another refinement in the garden. However she told me she intended to use Mr. Postlethwaite, a retired employee from Atkinson's, to do the garden work.

Progress was painfully slow as Mr. Postlethwaite experienced most of the ailments of old age and had many days off. There also seemed to be a lot of digging in the flower-beds which didn't seem to have anything to do with the new steps or path. On one occasion when I went to the house, I noticed that part of the terrace was being dug up. When I asked about this, Mrs. A said it was not my concern and told me to get on with my work.

One day as I arrived, Mrs. Atkinson said with pride, "Now John, I have something to show you. Follow me!"

She marched me through the kitchen, through the washroom, through the back door and out onto the terrace. I realised the garden project must be finished.

She walked to the back of the terrace by the house. Here there was an outside tap and a hosepipe running from it under the paving on the terrace.

"Now watch the garden," she said.

Slowly as the hosepipe filled, a shower of water rose

into the air. It formed an arch over the path and landed mostly on the beds and lawn on the other side.

I realised that my new circuit for testing the raincoats would be permanently wet.

"Do you like it?" asked Mrs. Atkinson with delight. "We won't be dependent on our unreliable climate for consistent or predictable rain."

I grudgingly agreed that I understood but at the same time I felt I was becoming something of a laboratory animal. Mrs. Atkinson was clearly disappointed in my lack of enthusiasm.

"Well, whether you like it or not, you are going to walk through it to test the new tape adhesives. We will start at lunchtime!"

"Time to put on your things, John," said Mrs. Atkinson at 12.30.

"What about lunch, Mrs. Atkinson," I countered as I was already getting hungry.

"I thought it would be better if you did your first excursion before you deserve any lunch!"

Clearly Glynis was still peeved at my lack of enthusiasm at the new rain-making arrangements and was getting her own back by making me wait for my lunch.

I went into the cloakroom to change into the clothes I would wear under the raincoat. I had learned how to put on the bra without any help and been provided with a couple of balloons filled with paste as fillers. These did provide a satisfactory wobble inside the bra.

Then came the roll-on girdle with suspenders, which I could now position pretty well. I had also learned how to put on the stockings without laddering them. I had to keep my toenails short. The arrangement was if I laddered the nylon stockings I would have to pay for the replacements out of my wages. So I was very careful as I had learned they were not cheap.

Mrs. Atkinson had given me a cream blouse of hers made in a very thin material so that I could feel the smoothness of the rubberised raincoat through it. It had short sleeves so I could feel the rubber directly against the skin of my lower arms.

Then came the deportment slip which Mrs A insisted I wore on this occasion. As I had not worn it before for this operation, I hoped there would be enough room inside it for me to get up the steps.

I now had a pair of medium high heels. The heels were quite blocky. This meant they would not sink into gaps between the flagstones on the terrace, or indeed into the gravel path when it was wet.

While I was getting ready I could hear some banging and crashing of what sounded like cutlery and crockery in the kitchen. As I returned I saw Mrs. A was filling a couple of hessian shopping bags with cutlery from the drawers and plates from the cupboards.

I didn't say anything but went towards the washroom which had become the dressing room. Mrs. A followed me carrying the two shopping bags.

The raincoat to be tested was a cross between royal blue and navy blue in colour. I knew Atkinson's sold a lot of them to school outfitters and institutions. They could be worn with most uniforms as an acceptable alternative to the shapeless gaberdine coats that were inflicted on pupils of all ages.

It was simple in design, single-breasted and pulled in at the waist with a sturdy belt. Mrs. A liked to dress me in the coats so she could arrange them to look their best.

"Breathe in," she said and then gave the belt an extra jerk to pull it a notch tighter.

"Put on your gloves," she said.

The gloves she was referring to were sturdy rubber washing gloves which it was becoming necessary for ladies to use while washing up or doing household laundry. In years gone by such things were done by servants but now that ladies increasingly had to do these things for themselves, they needed to protect their hands.

"Now to make this as realistic as possible, you can carry these two shopping bags. And to make sure you don't drop them we will secure them with this."

She pulled a ball of thick string and a pair of scissors out of one of the bags. She cut a couple of lengths.

Then she slid the strings through the handles of each of the bags, wound them a couple of times around my wrist, knotting each at the back of each wrist.

Then she pulled down the sleeves to below my wrist level and pulled the wristlet belts at the bottom of the sleeves tight. These were designed to stop water running up or blowing up your sleeves. However they also had the effect of sealing me into the coat as I could not see or reach my wrists.

Next she did up the top button of the coat and pulled up the high collar.. Then she put on the "neck strap'. This was something she had developed at the request of some headmistresses. They had said that some of their older girls had the habit of looking at the ground in front of them as they walked and this was not at all the kind of deportment they wanted to develop in well turned-out young ladies.

So Mrs. Atkinson had come up with a wide navy blue neck strap with a rectangular buckle which fastened under the chin. This meant the wearer had to keep their head up to keep their chin off the buckle which would otherwise press down painfully on the breast bone.

She supplied these 'neck straps' as an optional extra with the raincoats for girls who needed to improve their posture.

Needless to say Mrs. Atkinson pulled the neck strap to the tightest hole so the buckle went securely between my chin and breastbone. Now I could only see the ground from about three feet ahead and could not look down to see my feet.

Then she pulled up the hood from the back and over my head quite firmly. She pulled it well forward so I could not see to either side and crossed the strings under my chin, across the buckle of the neck strap, and tied them in a double knot at the back of my neck. I felt like a prisoner in my raincoat. The only thing I could do was move forward with small steps.

"You are ready, off you go." She picked up a big wooden spoon which must have had something to do with the washing and delivered a quick thwack across my thinly covered bottom. I gave an involuntary jerk and I am sure I heard her make a quiet sound of satisfaction.

She opened the back door for me and I shuffled forward.

"Mind the step," she said with a light laugh.

Because of my imprisonment in my hood and the tightly pulled neck strap, I had to feel gingerly with the soles of my shoes to get over the back door lip. I found it best to go down from the back doorstep sideways.

Slowly I felt my way forward one step at a time towards the edge of the terrace. Mrs. Atkinson took my arm and guided me towards the edge of the terrace.

"Stop there," she said. Then she went back to turn on the water.

As I stood on the edge of the terrace, with my limited field of vision from inside my hood and the two heavy bags tied to my wrists, I felt even more that I had become like her mechanical doll.

Suddenly the water jets rose into the air as Mrs. A opened the tap more and more.

"Off you go," she said.

I hesitated at plunging into the plumes of water and

was rewarded by another thwack across the bottom with the wooden spoon. Because of my hood and neck strap, I could not look down at the steps. But to avoid another thwack, I turned sideways and put one foot over the edge gingerly and started my journey.

Going down in my tight deportment slip was not too difficult. The steps were slightly more than one foot wide.

Once down on the path I could step out a bit more confidently, but not very far each time. The deportment slip severely restricted the size of my step. At first I thought I had to hurry but I found it was better to slow down and go for a steady rhythm.

Now I had a bit of time to feel what I was experiencing. There was a gentle even pattering of water drops onto my hood and upper body. Because of the thin blouse I could distinctly feel the droplets on my back, shoulders and arms.

As I was approaching the steps back to the terrace, there was a slight upward incline and I really felt the restriction around my knees. I arrived at the steps with some uncertainty that I would be able to get up them. Gingerly I stepped onto the first step. I lifted my leg for the next step and found it didn't quite have enough room. Then I remembered from somewhere that I had seen a girl in a tight skirt put her leg out to the side rather than straight in front when going up some stairs to get a bit more height. I tried this and it worked.

I did this on the next step with the other leg and realised I had only one more to go! Then I looked up to see Mrs. A standing at the top of the steps with her hands on her hips. She had a mischievous look on her face. She was obviously enjoying my discomfiture.

As I reached the top of the steps she took a pace back and signaled for me to turn to the left to go along the terrace.

"Round again," she said. She walked alongside me and delivered a gentler tap on my bottom with the wooden spoon. She was obviously quite pleased with the way it was going. When we got to the steps down she told me to stop and turn.

I asked her somewhat truculently, "How many times do I have to do this?"

"Until I tell you to stop!" she snapped back and this time there was nothing gentle about the thwack I received across the bottom. I heard her stomp across the terrace, go through the back door and close it after her.

Now I had no choice but to keep going and do my best to enjoy the experience. After all, a few months ago I would have regarded this as my ultimate fantasy.

Here I was wearing women's underclothes, stockings, high heels and on top of it all a rubberised raincoat buttoned up to the chin and walking in guaranteed rain.

The temperature inside the coat had now risen to match my body temperature. It was very pleasant to feel the cold droplets hitting the outside of the raincoat but they didn't make me feel cold. Inside my hood my head and hair were dry and because of the limited movement of my legs, my feet didn't catch more than the occasional drop of water.

However as I passed the kitchen window I saw Mrs. A looking out at me. She was pointing at her shoulders indicating I should hold my shoulders back more. I noticed also that she was chewing in a way intended for me to notice. I had forgotten that I was hungry with the other rigours I was now experiencing.

My shoulders were beginning to hurt with the weight of the shopping bags. Also the water vapour had coagulated to put a drip on the end of my nose. Because of the bags I could not brush it off with my hand and wiggling my nose didn't cause it to fall.

My legs too were beginning to ache with working so

hard inside the restriction of the deportment slip. In addition there was a warm glow on my bottom from the wooden spoon which I would have liked to relieve by rubbing with my hand. However, I didn't have a hand to spare!

I lost track of how many times I had been round. When I struggled up the steps for maybe the tenth or twelfth time, I was pleased to see that Mrs. A was standing there. She had put on her own raincoat, presumably because of the water mist drifting across the terrace. It was Shiny Black Rubber, neatly nipped in at the waist with a wide belt. It made her look quite intimidating, which was no doubt her intention. In her hand she had the wooden spoon. She signaled for me to turn left along the terrace. She walked beside me. I fully expected the wooden spoon on my already sore bottom again, but fortunately it didn't come.

"Have you had enough?"

"Yes thank you, Mrs. Atkinson," I said in a much more chastened tone of voice.

"Are you sure you wouldn't like to go round a few more times?"

"No Mrs. Atkinson, please," I said in a pleading voice.

"Stop there," she said and went to turn off the water.

As she released me from my bondage, Mrs. Atkinson said, "Well let this be a lesson to you. There is only one person round here who calls the tune."

"Yes Mrs. Atkinson," I said quickly.

For good or for ill, this was the day that Mrs. Atkinson discovered that she enjoyed putting me at a physical disadvantage. She had found she liked to have me trussed up in restrictive clothing to do her bidding. She also enjoyed causing me a little physical discomfort and even pain. She liked the way she could use these things to make me more compliant and obedient to her wishes.

The episode ended happily as inspection of the

seams showed no water penetration and I was allowed to have my lunch wearing the silver raincoat (now grey) that Mrs. Atkinson had given me to wear whilst at her house.

11

In The Studio

"I have been thinking. How would you like to model some of our raincoats?" Mrs. Atkinson said a few days later.

"If you think I could. How would that be possible?" I asked in bewilderment.

"Well when I dressed you up the other day, I saw that you could stand well and hold a pose. Those raincoats from our so-called competitors have got some stylish features of merit. We could do with copying them into some of our designs. In fact we need some radical new designs to beat off those upstarts. Did you know I used to do fashion drawing quite well?"

"No Mrs. Atkinson," I said, but I was beginning to realise that she had many more qualities and talents than I could ever have guessed.

"Well you could pose for me wearing these new coats. I can draw them and then I can draw some new designs to be made up by our samples department If you do well you can model the new coats for me to draw and I can send them to the advertising agency for finishing.

"Ask your mother if you can stay late next Tuesday evening and we can make a start then."

I couldn't wait until Tuesday. Mrs. Atkinson had a very strong work ethic and she would not stop doing her normal work until 5.30, which was the time that work finished at the factory. At 5.30 we finished for the day and she made us a cup of tea which we had with a piece of fruitcake. That was one the many perks of working at Mrs. Atkinson's house. I got to taste luxuries which did not normally come my way.

While we were sitting in the kitchen having our cup of tea, Mrs. Atkinson briefed me.

"I have cleared some space in the best-lit corner of the dining room. You will have a space to stand in the light and I can sit at the dining table and draw you.

"Once we get a pose right, I will want you to hold it for at least ten minutes so I can draw all the details. Can you manage that?"

"I am sure I can Mrs. Atkinson," I said, not knowing if I could but knowing that a positive attitude was the only acceptable response to Mrs. A.

"I have already collected your underclothes in the dining room and put your knickers and bra at the bottom of the stairs. Take them into the cloakroom and put them on. Then come quietly to the dining room, and knock. We don't want to disturb Mrs. Atkinson Senior."

When I had done as she asked, Mrs. A opened the door and let me into the dining room. I had only seen this room in daylight when I was bringing information to Mrs. Atkinson or had been called in to answer a question. Now it was so different. The curtains were drawn and the wall lights gave the room a completely different atmosphere. The gas fire had been lit and the room was already quite warm.

The table where Mrs. Atkinson worked by the window had been cleared and the ornaments that normally covered the dining table had been moved onto it. Now the dining table contained only a table light with Mrs. A's drawing board, and her pencils and pens.

"Makes quite a nice studio, don't you think?"

"Yes Mrs. Atkinson," I replied.

"Now come over to the fire and stop shivering."

I hadn't realised that I was shivering and was glad to come close to the warm fire. It was nice standing in front of it feeling the gentle heat on my legs.

"Let us see how much you remember from last time. I have some new underclothes for you that you may need some help with."

I did need help with a couple of things. Each time she did something for me she made me undo it and do it again until I could do each stage on my own.

"I don't want to be dressing you every time, big girls can dress themselves!"

I liked the idea of being a big girl who was able to dress herself in these lovely-feeling clothes.

"I don't want you to put on your restrictive deportment slip today. I want you to wear this instead."

She held up what looked initially like a white gym bag but when I looked at it more closely I saw it was a pair of knickers. However they seemed to be full of something soft and lumpy.

"You may have a divine figure," said Mrs. A, "but it doesn't look realistic for a grown woman. We need to give you some hips and bottom."

She held open the lumpy item and I could see there were spaces for me to put my legs through. I stepped into the padded pants and pulled them up. They felt strange of course but the extra bulk around the hips made me feel more feminine.

"Now another new thing we need to do is give you a more feminine shape round the middle. We need to cinch in your ribs just above your waist. And this little devil should do that for you."

She produced a short corset which she said was a rib corset.

"Oh dear," she exclaimed, "we are getting ahead of ourselves. You will have to take off the padded pants first so you can slide the corset over your natural bottom and hips."

When I took off the padded pants I realised how snug and warm they were on top of my thin knickers. I realised they already felt part of me. The corset was already threaded with long laces which had been loosened to allow it to go over my hips. Once in position, Mrs. A turned it so the laces were at the back and began to tighten them.

"Breathe out as I pull," she said. As I did so I felt the corset contract around my lower ribs.

"And again," came the instruction. Then I realised I couldn't breathe so far down into my lungs because of the restriction. Mrs. A gave one more pull then said, "That is as far as it will go for the moment. You probably won't be able to cope with it for more than an hour the first time, but that should be long enough."

I felt I had a completely different torso. Not only did I have a false bosom but below it I had this narrowing ribcage with an even more reduced waist as this is where the laces were tied. Then from below my waist I had my new protruding hips and, I presumed, a well-formed bottom at the back.

"One more thing we need to do is to deal with your slouching shoulders," said Mrs. A. "You have improved a little, but only when you remember. So I have devised something which will remind you."

She picked up something which seemed to be made of wide white strapping. She told me to put my arms out at the back. She then slipped the contraption up my arms and over my shoulders. It formed two loops over the top of my shoulders and these were joined by straps at the back. Then I felt Mrs. Atkinson adjust one of the back straps to tighten it and pull my shoulders back further.

I felt like a trussed chicken but realised that all these restraining contrivances would be hidden under my outer clothes.

"Now put on this dress," said Mrs. A. "Arms up!"

She rolled up and dropped over my head and arms what turned out to be a short floral dress that came to just above my knees. She zipped up the side and fastened the buckled belt.

"Now let me look at you," Mrs. Atkinson said. "Turn round slowly."

After a few moments' appraisal she said, "Now that's what I would call a figure."

"Thank you, Mrs. Atkinson," I said. I realised with the lower rib constriction I could only speak with half the normal amount of breath. So my voice came out softer and lighter than usual.

"Now for shoes, you can wear something a bit higher as you won't be walking. Try these on." She passed me a pair of black court shoes with narrow, almost stiletto heels.

"I have put a small rug in the area I want you to stand on, so you won't mark the wooden floor. You had better sit down on the dining room chair closest to the rug so that you can stand and step onto your rug."

The area she had chosen was in the corner of the room close to one of the wall lights. She had also directed a standard light from near the fireplace to illuminate the same area. So I had light falling on me from several directions, which minimised the shadows.

I sat rigidly upright on the edge of my chair. That was all I could do. My shoulder brace was beginning to hurt. The only way I could give myself some relief was to pull my shoulders even further back. It surprised me how far back my shoulders would go.

"Right, stand up," she instructed. I slowly lifted myself onto my high heels. After steadying myself I took one single step onto my rug.

From the other corner of the room Mrs. Atkinson brought the first of the upstart competitors' coats. It was the Lilac one, which was the first one I had worn outside to test its waterproofness.

Although she wanted me to be more independent, I

think she did enjoy dressing me and arranging my clothes. I of course did enjoy being dressed by her. With my new height I was actually a fraction taller than she was in the normal low-heeled shoes she wore around the house.

She helped me with the delicious swathes of lilac fabric that made up this coat.. The top was quite close-fitting then flared out from the waist.

Mrs. A made me do the buttons up myself, almost down to the hem. Then she started to adjust the belt. "I think we will take the belt off the dress. It is preventing us getting the smoothest fit around your waist."

So the buttons had to be undone again. Then Mrs. A fished around my waist to free the dress belt from its loops. It was wonderful to have her touch me. She was so close I could smell her scent – what we called perfume in those days. It mixed with the smell of the rubberised inside of the coat and was a heady mix indeed. I thought I was going to faint with pleasure!

"There, now button yourself up again," she said.

Now she was able to get the belt to fit to her satisfaction. Then she carefully arranged the pleats of the skirt of the coat as I slowly turned around under her instructions.

"Do you know why these top-of-the-range raincoats have a full skirt like this one?"

"No Mrs. Atkinson," I said. "I hadn't really thought about it. I suppose because it's the fashion."

"Well there is a very practical reason. There is no point in a lady being dry and warm above but walking in soaking wet shoes, is there?"

"Oh I see, it's to keep her feet dry!"

"Exactly, the fullness of the skirt drops the running water beyond the space the lady walks in.

"That is why capes are so sensible. Wearing one is like walking in a rubberised tent. The circle of the hem of the cape is so large it drops the water well beyond the area of your feet as you walk."

That was in the days before women's boots had been reinvented as a fashion item. The only boots that women had access to then were shapeless fur-lined ankle boots. Fashionable women would not wish to be seen in that kind of boot, except maybe in deep snow!

"I like the buttons going down to the bottom too," said Mrs. Atkinson.

"It prevents the coat blowing open at the bottom in the wind."

She clearly had a very good eye for detail.

"I have taken the hood off for now as I want to be able to get a clear view of the back of the coat and the collar."

As she pulled up the collar, I realised it overlapped at the front and had a hidden button to hold it closed. The result was that the collar came halfway up the side of the face and passed just below the nose.

"Nice touch that," she said to herself. "Wait a minute while I find you a suitable hat."

While she had gone I thought to myself, "I have never been upstairs but she must have several wardrobes full of clothes and hats and shoes."

Soon she was back with a brimmed hat. It was the sort of hat that Marlene Dietrich and Ingrid Bergman had worn in films during and after the war.

Finally Mrs. A showed me how to stand.

"The thing to remember with high heels is that they throw your weight forward. So you must remember to pull your tummy in so that that you remain straight and elegant.

"We will go for a simple pose first. Left foot forward as if you are walking and body turned very slightly towards me. Arms loosely down by your sides. No, you need a bag," she said and was off again.

I had an image of more shopping bags full of cutlery and crockery. When Mrs. A came back she had several handbags. She finally decided on a simple envelope bag which I had to hold under my left armpit and that brought my left hand up to just above my waist.

"Yes that's good. Hold that!

"Pity we haven't got a full-length mirror for you to see yourself."

I would like to have seen myself but the only mirror in the room was above the fireplace.

"In fact I could almost use you as a photographic model," she said, more to herself than to me, but without much conviction.

Mrs. A got going on her drawing with relish. I could see her hand moving slowly for short periods but she spent most of the time looking at me.

"Look twice as long as you draw was what I was taught," she said but I could tell from her tone that she didn't need an answer.

Once the outline was done, drawing of the long bold lines was followed by cross hatching and shading. I did not find it hard standing still for what I suppose was about 15 minutes.

"Good, that will do for that one." I was relieved because I was just beginning to get uncomfortable.

"Now, turn around slowly until I tell you to stop… stop!! Can you move your weight onto your right leg so it pushes your right hip up?"

I was unable to do it satisfactorily so she had to come and show me. She said it moved the weight to one side and that made the back of the coat ripple in an interesting way.

I spent another ten minutes in that position. Fortunately, just as I was beginning to get uncomfortable, Mrs. A changed the pose. I realised she could tell by tiny physical movements when I had had enough. She told me later that she had life drawing lessons in Paris before the war and the students learned they had to move quickly before the model lost the natural hold on their pose. They could tell when the muscles were starting to strain. Presumably those models were nude but Mrs. A could tell even when the model was fully dressed.

"That is enough for that raincoat," she announced. "You can move around now and loosen up, but don't move off your mat."

I shook my shoulders and felt the fabric of this wonderful coat move against my upper body. I put down my bag on the chair. Then I put my hands in the pockets and moved the skirt of the coat so that it rustled and swished around my legs.

"Remind me to show you there is a way that a lady puts her hands in her raincoat pockets which is much more graceful than the way you do it," said Mrs. A as she put a couple more marks on the drawing.

"But not now," she said standing up. "It is time for our showpiece yellow coat. Undo your belt and buttons but don't step off your mat."

I was beginning to feel like Nelson on top of his column. I didn't dare step over the edge.

Mrs. A slipped off the lilac raincoat and I suddenly lost its pleasant shrouding warmth. Then she put me into a wonderful tent of daffodil-yellow rubberised fabric. I thought the colour was like sunshine. The generous smooth rubber of the wide sleeves felt wonderful against my bare arms.

The daffodil-yellow raincoat had a swagger back. This hung loose to swish and swirl as one moved. I noticed with pleasure that it also had a hood that I would be able to hide my head in.

"Do up your buttons while I go and check on Mrs.

Atkinson," said Mrs. A.

These buttons were more awkward because they were fly-fronted, that is, covered over by a strip of fabric down the front, like the front of a pair of men's trousers. This coat was completely different because it didn't have any waist, as far as I could see.

"This is a very cleverly designed raincoat," said Mrs. A on her return as she inspected my buttons, which again went down nearly to the hem. She explained to me that this was the latest fashion.

"Not only are the buttons invisible, but the coat can be worn in three ways.

"First, it can be loose as we have it now. Second, we can give it a normal shape by putting this belt round the waist. The third way is feed the belt through this slit in this side seam and out again on the other side."

Once again I had the pleasure of Mrs. A feeling around my waist to pass the belt back out through the other slit. She then fastened the belt at the front. I could feel the belt against my back inside the raincoat but performing no function but to pull in the front of the coat. I could feel the raincoat billowing out behind me like a cloud that would follow me.

"That looks very chic!" said Mrs. A as she made me swirl around on my mat. The rustle of the coat was almost deafening and I felt as if I was inside a rubber waterfall. Then Mrs. A arranged my pose and started to draw.

Once again we did a front view and a back view. While standing there I realised that as this coat flared out from the shoulders, rather than the waist, there was a lot of fabric around the hem. This will protect my feet at the back but not at the front, I thought. Then I thought that it wouldn't always be raining but it might be windy. That would be the ideal time to wear the belt like this to prevent the whole coat filling with wind. I imagined walking in this coat in the wind with the back billowing and flapping out behind me like a sail.

"Now turn halfway round to your right," said Mrs. Atkinson. "Then turn your head and shoulders towards me. Now hold your bag back against the fold of the coat and put your other hand partly into the pocket."

I noticed for the first time that this coat had two big patch pockets with flaps.

"Very useful to keep things in," I thought.

After a few more adjustments, she began to draw again.

Finally we did the orange raincape. I was beginning to flag by then and noticed my rib corset was indeed beginning to hurt. It was however fun to be covered in this cape of such lovely rippling rubberised fabric. It felt much nicer against my arms and the backs of my hands than ordinary sleeves. I supposed this was because I could move them against the fabric more.

There were slits in each side and Mrs. A had me with one arm extending out from one of the slits to touch one of the buttons, as if I was fastening it.

"Very nice," she said at last. "That will do for this evening."

"May I see the drawings Mrs. Atkinson?" I asked.

"Oh no! These are only the rough sketches. It will take me a lot longer to do the finished ink drawings. You may see those when I am happy with them.

"Now we must get you out of those things and home to your mother."

On my way to the bus stop I was 'walking on air', imagining myself still wearing those lovely coats.

12

The Price of Beauty

It was at least a week later when Mrs. Atkinson showed me the first of her ink drawings based on our lovely evening in the dining room.

"Yes, I am quite pleased with the way you posed for me and the fact that I seem to have recovered some of my skills. Mind you, these are not the first drawings. It took several attempts to get them anything like right."

To my eyes they were perfect.

"They are better than any pictures I have seen in advertisements," I said.

"That is very kind of you John, but they are not that good. I would have to give them to a finishing artist to produce the final drawing if it was going to be used for press advertising. There is a lot more to it than you may think.

"One interesting thing to come out of it is that the hat you wore looked very good on you! I am sure we could design and make storm hats like that with a big brim in matching rubberised fabric. What do you think John?"

"That sounds very good. May I make a suggestion Mrs. Atkinson?"

"Yes, what is it?" she said without enthusiasm.

"It occurred to me that when a lady was wearing a raincape, like I did, she would get her arm very wet when she put it outside through the slit. What about making her matching gloves?"

"I will think about it," said Mrs. Atkinson absently.

"You know I would have to pay a lot of money to a professional model to wear those clothes so I could draw them. And I would have to go to a studio in Manchester.

More expense!

"So it is very useful to have someone to do it here at a time that is convenient to me.

"I can use these drawings as a base to design a new range. If the customers want glamour and fantasy, we are going to give it to them," she said with growing enthusiasm. I can improve on those designs. We can push back those interlopers to put Atkinson's back on top!"

She was clearly excited by the prospect of producing a new range of glamorous, chic rainwear in the new colourful fabrics that were becoming available.

"We will need to advertise in the press to tell our customers that we have a new range. I can do the drawings and the advertising agency can finish them before sending them to the newspapers and magazines.

"The trouble is that drawings will probably soon be replaced by photographs. I am told that is what the public want. Magazine publishing is becoming much more mechanised these days. They can publish colour pictures to a very high standard. Unfortunately the cost of getting good photographic models is very high and they usually end up not doing what you asked them to do and it all has to be done again. Then there is the cost of the studio! Illustrated drawings are so much easier."

I guessed she might be thinking about what she had said on the evening of the drawings. I judged it best not to say anything. I had a slight intuition of what was coming.

"Jo...hn," she stretched my name, "how would you like to become our photographic model for the new range of raincoats we are working on?"

I knew that if Mrs. A actually asked me something rather than told me, it was a rare moment of uncertainty. Of course I loved the prospect of doing it. Although I may have had my own doubts, I knew I needed to be decisive. Otherwise she might think better of the idea.

"If you think I could do it, Mrs. Atkinson, then I'm sure I could."

"Right then," she said decisively.

"You will have to work hard on looking more feminine, especially your face and hair, and your hands."

"Yes Mrs. Atkinson," I said. "But what about my mother? She is bound to notice."

"Don't worry about your mother. She and I have a good understanding. I am sure I can reassure her. Anyway she has much more pressing things to concern her.

"Actually I have decided that Mrs. Atkinson should go into a nursing home. She is getting too much work for me and Mrs. Holroyd. The General Hospital won't have her because unfortunately they say they can't do any more for her than I can. She will be much more comfortable in the nursing home up the road. I can visit her every day.

"Anyway that means you can stay here sometimes and have your own room to practice in. This house is enormous and I have to stay here for the moment because it is the Atkinson family home."

This was my first indication that Glynis had some sort of personal plan for the future. Meanwhile my head was reeling with the possibilities for my own future.

"You will have to start looking after your skin better.

"And stop shaving. You hardly need to shave but the longer you hold off, the longer you can keep your beard at bay. I can deal with the few wispy hairs you have coming through.

"We will have to find you a hairstyle that will do for when you are a girl and a boy. You will have to come with me dressed as a girl to a ladies' hairdresser. Could you cope with that?

"And then there are your eyebrows. They will have to be trimmed and plucked.

"But I can do that for you," she made this last

statement with a little relish in her voice. I had yet to find out why.

"Then you will have to learn how to put on make-up. You won't need much because your skin is in good condition. The trick will be to make it look as if you aren't wearing any. At your age you can get away with that.

"Are you ready for all this?" she asked in conclusion.

I took a deep breath and said, "I am, sure I am," even though I wasn't.

"That's my ...girl," she said and giggled like someone half her age.

Within a few weeks things started to change. Mrs. Atkinson Senior was moved out to the nearby nursing home and Glynis was visibly under less stress.

I now started to live to a new regime. I still went up to the house in the afternoons but now I stayed overnight on a couple of evenings. I still arrived at the factory at the same time, even though I came on a different bus from a different direction. Mrs. A said it was important that they did not know at the office about our arrangements and plans. Needless to say my mother had been informed and presumably had raised no objection.

After a few weeks I began to wonder why Glynis still worked mostly from home when she no longer had to look after Mrs. Atkinson Senior. I suppose she had built such a good reporting system to control the business from a distance that she no longer needed to be there every day.

She still continued to work conscientiously through the day as she had always done. However she now did much more of the things she enjoyed. She was able to spend time designing and drawing. She would also spend time drawing out patterns for the prototype designs.

After I arrived with her statistics, reports and business mail, I had my own routine. I went to the bedroom Mrs. A had allocated to me. There I had to change into the clothes she had given me. These were a white bra with my paste-filled balloons, white knickers, roll-on girdle with suspenders and nylon stockings. Also I had to wear my restrictive underskirt, which Glynis had taken in even further. Actually she made no allowances for my restriction and liked to see me trot when she called me. She said it made me look like an efficient secretary.

On top of these underclothes I wore a white blouse and a black pencil skirt. On cold days I also wore a black cardigan which was provided for me from Glynis's vast wardrobe. This outfit was what I wore almost all the time when I was at the house, like a uniform. Well I suppose that as I was her secretary that was appropriate.

The only variables were the shoes. I started with low chunky heels. Each day I had deportment lessons walking up and down the hall. Every few weeks a different pair of shoes appeared. The heels got higher and I had to get used to wearing them and walking in them. As Mrs. Atkinson used to say, a lady needs to be able to look as if she was born to walk in high heels!

At first Mrs. A used to put on my make-up, then gradually I was able to do it for myself. I was also taught how to take it off at nights and put on night cream to keep my skin moist.

I also had lessons in speaking in a light falsetto voice. I was told not to belch or do any of the things teenage boys do to deepen their voices. Mrs. A also made me work on my pronunciation.

She would ask me to read out loud to her. Sometimes I would repeat the same sentence or phrase many times until she was satisfied with my pronunciation. I had thought my voice was alright and it never occurred to me that I might have an accent. Sometimes we used to listen to the radio in the evenings and she would ask me to pay particular attention to the way some people spoke. I would then have to read something in what she called my BBC voice.

Once a week I had to endure a more challenging experience. This was my hair removal session. Mrs. A had forbidden shaving and my wispy hair growth had to be removed. The first session had been something of a disaster. I had not been ready for the pain involved in having hair removed with a pair of tweezers. I jumped about and wriggled so much that Mrs. Atkinson had to abandon the session and I was quite close to tears.

Needless to say, Mrs. Atkinson was not prepared to give up. She informed me that if I wanted to live my dream of being a plausible woman, I would have to get used to pain on the way. She said she had devised a way of making it less painful for me but it would still hurt a bit. Would I be brave?

Her solution was to make it more of a game. What the session consisted of was me sitting on a sturdy chair with my hands tied to the sides and my legs tied together. Then she placed one of her rubber-lined capes over me and the chair and buttoned me at the back. The cape was a deep plum colour and had a detachable hood. She told me I would find the hair removal less painful if my skin pores were opened by perspiration. To cause this she would pull the rubber hood up over my head and tie the drawstring at the back. She said she would leave the hood over my head for about 20 minutes and that would induce a nice sweat that would open the pores all over my face. We experimented with tying the hood to balance the ability of it to induce a sweat and to allow in enough air for me to breathe. Although my head was fully enclosed by the hood, and I was in total darkness, there were some gaps at the bottom where the hood was buttoned to the collar of the coat. This was where my air supply got in. Nevertheless I had to breathe deeply to create the pressure to push out the old air and let in the fresh air. I became quite adept at this.

To further induce a sweat we would do this in the kitchen with the chair placed near the coke-burning Aga range. Solid fuel burning ranges were highly desirable during the 1950s and Aga was the top brand. Because there was also likely to be sweat on my body, I had to take off my outer clothes and sit tied to the chair in my bra, girdle, knickers and stockings.

When the twenty minutes were up Mrs A would untie the hood and then came the painful bit. She would sit astride me on my knees and grip my thighs with hers. This meant she could just about keep me still with her weight when I wriggled. I tended to wriggle a lot as she pulled out the reluctant hairs from my face.

She had tried sitting sideways on but found she could not get such a good view and access to both sides of my face. Also on one occasion my movements had nearly caused her to fall on the floor.

Initially she would have to remove her own skirt and pull up her slip to do this.

Then she started to wear more suitable clothes, rather than the pencil skirt which was her normal attire.

Once the pores on my face got used to opening easily, we no longer needed the kitchen heat. Mrs. A decided it would be more convenient to move the whole operation upstairs. She would secure me to a chair in my room, inside my sweat-inducing cape and hood. Then from inside my hood I could hear her banging about in her own room, which was next door to mine. She was looking through her wardrobes and hat boxes for suitable clothes to wear for our session.

Sometimes she would wear trousers but on other occasions she wore evening dresses and even a full ball gown with a big net petticoat that tickled my legs, even through my stockings.

I found she seemed to enjoy the process. I didn't

know then but realise now she was indulging a slightly sadistic side of her nature. She seemed to enjoy my twitches of pain, while at the same time seeming to be sympathetic. Gripping me with her thighs and holding me down with her body weight must have given her a similar feeling to that which many women get from controlling a frisky pony.

Later she took to actually wearing riding jodhpurs. She told me she had used to ride a lot when she was younger but events of recent years had made it impossible. Sometimes she even put on her riding boots and a riding Mac.

Part of my excitement was that I did not know what vision would greet me when she untied my face covering hood.

For me the compensating benefit of the pain was being so close to the face and body of such a beautiful woman. I could do little but look in wonder into her eyes as she searched my face for wispy hairs to remove with her tweezers.

I didn't realise at the time but I had fallen completely in love with this woman!

It was of course a mixture of puppy love for a mother I had not really had, and my admiration for a beautiful sophisticated woman who was prepared to spend time and trouble grooming me to fulfill my fantasies.

The trouble was that this close proximity and my mixed-up feelings towards Mrs. Atkinson had predictable results. I became quite sexually aroused during these sessions and my manhood started to manifest itself. Her warm body close to mine and the stimulus of the rubber led to my developing a significant erection. I was of course embarrassed and hoped she would not notice.

After a while I realised that she knew perfectly well the effect she was having on me and enjoyed it all the more. She would actually push up against me with the apparent intention of getting closer to see my face better. I could feel the warmth of her groin against mine and that made my erection even sturdier.

After the hairs on my cheeks, we came to the eyebrows. She trimmed some but others had to be pulled out. This was a different level of pain, even after having a good sweat. Not only did I wriggle and writhe but I also let out yelps of pain.

Ever resourceful, Mrs. Atkinson evolved a solution. This was a makeshift rubber gag. It was made out of a rubber swimming hat which she stuffed with some old stockings and pushed into my mouth. Then she tied another stocking around my mouth to hold the gag in position. She told me if the plucking hurt, instead of screaming, I could bite on the gag.

Usually by the time we had done the hairs on my cheeks, my skin had cooled down and the pores had closed. So during plucking my eyebrows I had to have several more sessions with my head in the hood. My gag was not removed for these periods so now I found myself not only tied but gagged inside my enveloping rubber cape and hood. I found the best way of dealing with this restriction was to consciously relax and enjoy it.

I totally trusted Mrs. Atkinson not to put me in danger and I enjoyed being under her complete control. Looking back now those experiences were some of the most wonderful of my life!

13

A Day Out

Meanwhile my hair was growing and finally the day arrived for my visit to the hairdressers. Mrs. Atkinson had decided we would travel out of Brunley to an area where we were not known. So she made an appointment at a hairdresser in the next town along the valley, which was called Perston.

Fortunately it was a rainy day and so I could wear my raincoat hood up to go to the hairdresser. Actually I didn't have to expose myself to much public scrutiny on the journey there as we went in Mrs. Atkinson's car. We only had a short walk and Mrs. A allowed me to use an umbrella to hide behind.

I was under strict instructions to say as little as possible and let Mrs. A do the talking. She told me just to smile sweetly when people spoke to me but try not to say anything. She said they would assume I was shy.

Needless to say I had never been to a ladies' hairdressers before. As we went in, my stomach was churning and I walked as closely as I could behind Mrs. Atkinson.

I was not prepared for the strong smell which assailed my nostrils. I learned it was the smell of the stuff that is used for dyeing and perming hair. This was laced with some kind of scent. It made my stomach feel even queasier.

Mrs. A explained that I had been living in the country and had come to stay. Before I knew what had happened, my coat had been removed and I was swathed in a voluminous gown and dumped in a swivel chair.

Then I realised that the gown was rubber-backed. I

could feel it against the back of my hands and bare arms. This was some consolation in my predicament. I felt more protected and less vulnerable. Gradually a comforting rubber smell started to reach my nostrils and that started to overlay the other smells. I didn't know at the time what the reason was for this stroke of good fortune. Later I realised the gown was to prevent splashes of the foul smelling liquids getting onto the clothes of customers.

Then I was spun round and my head was leant backwards over a basin. I had no idea what was happening and then slowly realised this was so my hair could be washed from behind. What was a shock was how intimate it all was. The hairdresser's bosom was stuck in my face as she leant over me to rub shampoo into my hair and massage my scalp. She had an open blouse, similar to mine and I found myself trying not to breathe into the space between her breasts.

Fortunately Glynis sat close by and headed off attempts to ask me about where I came from, where I was going for my holidays, which film stars I fancied and other similar questions.

She decided what the length my hair was to be and the type of perm. I went through several further indignities and then found myself inside a whirring dome which I presumed was a dryer. Fortunately the level of noise was such that I was quite cut-off from everything and could not be asked questions.

After a while of being in my noisy cocoon of sound I began to wonder how long I would have to stay in there. My head was becoming quite warm and I hoped I had not been forgotten. Also the heat was building up inside my rubber lined gown. Fortunately I could move the air around by surreptitiously moving the gown around with my hands.

I turned my head as far as I could and saw Mrs. A reading a magazine. At that moment she looked up and smiled reassuringly. I smiled back weakly and sank gratefully back into my rubber cocoon!

Finally I was released from my hot encapsulation and accompanied back to the hairdresser for my curlers to be removed. I was appalled. My hair seemed to have been transformed into nothing but a series of tightly curled frizzed strands.

I was relieved to see the hairdresser brush out my hair into lovely waves. After several minutes' tweaking of my hair, I could not believe I was the person who was looking back at me from the mirror.

When it was finally finished, Mrs. Atkinson paid the bill and we walked out onto the pavement. The rain had stopped and there was no need to put up our hoods or for umbrellas. With my new hair I felt much more confident about standing in public view with Mrs. Atkinson next to me.

"What shall we do now?" she said. I knew better than to say anything.

"I know, we will go to the Royal Hotel for tea and spruce up our make-up."

She turned and started walking and I quickly caught up with her. Suddenly I felt awkward and clumsy. I didn't know what to do with my hands. I knew I daren't put them in my pockets which would pull my tightly belted raincoat out of shape.

As if reading my thoughts, Mrs. Atkinson said, "We will have to get you a handbag. Schoolgirls don't carry handbags but young ladies do."

I swelled with pride and found myself saying in my best feminine voice, "Ooh! Thank you!"

We stopped at a small shop and Mrs. A selected a very modest blue handbag to go with my navy raincoat. She also picked out a simple but serviceable purse for me. I duly thanked her, again in my most feminine voice. She seemed pleased.

Once again I was apprehensive about breaking new ground. Although I felt very safe with Mrs. A, I didn't want to embarrass her by making social mistakes. I had never been into a proper hotel before and had no idea what to expect. I thought you just went into a hotel when you were staying away from home, not that I ever had. I found myself even more intimidated by the prospect because as a result of my lessons in elocution and grammar, I had found out the correct way was to say 'an hotel' with the 'h' being silent.

As we arrived at the Royal Hotel, I was feeling quite queasy. We went up the steps and through a glass door. I followed very closely behind Mrs. A, trying to make myself invisible.

As we got through the door, my nose was assailed by a familiar smell. It was beer. I had occasionally been taken into the back room of our local pub by my Uncle Albert so I knew what the atmosphere of a pub was like. On one side of the hall was a bar filled with noisy lunchtime drinkers. As we passed the door I moved as close as possible to the opposite wall of the corridor and kept my eyes on the carpet just in front of me.

Mrs. A went serenely up to the reception desk and asked if we could have a pot of tea for two in the lounge. We turned away from the noisy bar and went into a large carpeted room with small tables and comfortable chairs. Fortunately there was nobody else in there.

"Shall we sit over here by the window?" asked Mrs. A. I knew I did not have to answer her but followed dumbly. Mrs. A unbuttoned her emerald green raincoat and slid it off with a magnificent swooshing sound, and laid it carefully over a chair.

"Take your raincoat off and put it on this chair," she said but her voice tailed off and didn't have its usual authority.

She did not sit down. "Come with me," she said.

Again I noticed her voice did not have its normal authority which she used when telling me what to do.

I started to follow her.

"Don't forget your handbag," she whispered over her shoulder. I realised I had left it on the chair with the coats. I turned clumsily to go back, almost knocking over a table.

Mrs. A was waiting for me by a door. As I approached her I suddenly realised what the door was and my heart skipped a beat and my face flushed. It was the ladies' toilet. Mrs. A went through the door and so I had to follow.

I felt like a criminal about to commit a crime. Inside I was pleased to say there was no one there but Mrs. Atkinson, who was examining her face in a big well-lit mirror.

"You had better use one of these, even if you don't need to go now," she said gesturing to the toilet cubicle doors.

I did as I was told. I was somewhat surprised to find it was much the same as a men's lavatory. The only exception was a white box at the side with the words "Sanitary Towels' emblazoned on it. I supposed I had better sit down to do what I had to do as that was more appropriate.

I listened carefully in case anyone else came in. Then I heard Mrs. A go into the cubicle next door. I waited until she had finished and gone back to the wash area before I dared to come out. As I sat there I realised that although it was similar to a men's toilet, it had its own smell. I wondered if they used different kinds of soap to clean women's toilets.

When I came out, Mrs. A had her handbag open and was powdering her face.

"You had better do the same. Your make-up got a little disturbed in the hairdresser's," she said. Again there was some hesitancy in the way she spoke to me.

As if reading the question in my mind she said, "I think I know what the problem is. I don't have a name to call you when we are out. I obviously can't call you John."

I wished she wouldn't say my name so loud.

"We will have to come up with a girl's name for you. What about Jane or Joanna? You choose!"

It was very rare for Mrs. A to give a real choice. I was pleased she had given me a choice on something so important. I chose Joanna!

"Good," she said. "You can call me Auntie when we are in public."

"Yes…Auntie," I said hesitantly.

Back in the lounge our tea had arrived. It was served on a silver tray and next to the table was a triple-shelved table with sandwiches, cakes and biscuits laid out on each shelf.

"Now watch carefully how I serve the tea. One day you will have to do it." This marked the beginning of my education into the ways of well brought up people.

After we had settled to eat our sandwiches and drink our tea, Mrs. Atkinson started to relax and talk in a way I had never heard her do before. She started to talk about things we might do and places we might go. She asked me if I liked to go to the pictures. She asked if I liked the theatre and when I told her I had never been, she was sympathetic but said nothing more.

As we finished our tea Mrs. A taught me that it was not ladylike to eat everything that was offered. She also showed me how to hold my fingers when drinking tea and how to wipe my fingers with the serviette.

As we returned home in the car, Mrs. A continued to talk about some of the places we might go to on visits. There were local landmarks, museums and interesting buildings to see.

I realised a little later this was the beginning of the

freedom that Glynis could see opening up for her now she no longer had to look after Mrs. Atkinson Senior for 24 hours a day.

It was also for me the beginning of an education into the manners of a world I had never experienced. In addition it was the beginning of my education about etiquette and behaviour. This was of vital importance for advancement beyond what might be expected for someone with my social origins.

14

The Fashion Shoot

The day of the fashion shoot was fast approaching. Mrs. Atkinson was busy getting the range of coats, capes and hats ready for me to model. I could feel the tension rising in her as the day approached.

She even put me on a special diet. It was not my figure, which was pretty stick-like and still needed padding around the hips and boobs. I was very proud of my slim waist which could be cinched to 18 inches. This was very important for the 'small waist, big skirt look' that Mrs. Atkinson still favoured.

The diet was for my complexion. I was not allowed to eat bread or potatoes. As my body was beginning to mature I had had one or two skin blemishes. This must not be allowed to happen for the Big Day. I had to cleanse and moisturise several times a day.

The hair removal session was on the day before the photo shoot. It was very thorough and there was no question of any fun and games. I was also sent to bed early for several nights so I would look my best.

The day before the shoot, Mrs. Atkinson and I went down to the studio. I was introduced to the photographer as Mrs. Atkinson's niece who was to be the model. I got the impression that the photographer was not too pleased at having to use this inexperienced girl rather than one of his usual models.

Our main purpose for going was to check the samples that had been delivered from the factory that morning. I knew they would be on time and right, if Mr. Wilkinson had had anything to do with it. We also had to hang them up overnight so that they would be in perfect condition for the next day.

Then it was home for a light tea and early to bed. The next morning I was awoken by Mrs. A before dawn for a final inspection for rogue hairs and undisciplined eyebrows. These were dealt with unceremoniously. That morning she made me up herself. She explained she was just doing the basics now and would complete the job at the studio. When I looked in the mirror I saw the result was unbelievable. When I thanked her and complimented her, I barely got a smile.

What I didn't know at the time was that she had stretched the finances of the company to the limit to pay for developing and launching this new collection of glamorous rainwear. She was therefore under quite a lot of stress to ensure all went well and right.

Her aim was to put Atkinson's on the map as a Rainwear Design House with an international reputation. Fortunately I didn't realise how important my role was in all this. In order to economise, Mrs. A had decided to use me as the model and not let the advertising agency charge her exorbitant amounts for organising the photography. Had I known, I might have considered it a false economy.

I was told to put on a simple dress and my everyday blue raincoat and school hat. Mrs. A looked stunning in a two-piece mauve suit which showed off her figure to great advantage. Around her shoulders she had a fur stole and on her head she had a small hat with a veil.

She never missed an opportunity to dress up and as usual, despite my butterflies, I was entranced.

Glynis Atkinson and I had become regular cinemagoers after I started to live at her house. If necessary we would travel considerable distances in her car to see the films that interested her. Many of the films had beautiful, languorous women like Greta Garbo and Marlene Dietrich.

She also liked the modern film idols like Ava Gardner and Jane Russell.

Gradually I realised that these were the icons on which she based her image. I was even more entranced to find that I was able to be in the company of someone whom I thought was the next best thing to a film star.

I didn't have much time to compliment her that morning but managed to say something complimentary as the car drove down the hill. I was rewarded with a gentle touch on the thigh from her gloved hand and a barely audible thank you. I sensed she didn't want to talk but wanted to think through the things that had to be done. This gave me a chance to relish the warmth on my thigh where she had touched me. I could feel that touch of her hand all the way into Manchester.

First stop was the hairdressers. Glynis had booked me in with a top-name salon to have my hair styled for the shoot. We had visited the same salon the week before to have a trim and colour.

Exactly on time at 11 am, Mrs. A and I made our entrance into the studio. I was surprised at the transformation. The previously dull studio area was now bathed in light and furnished with a variety of props and scenery to be used in the photography.

The attitude of the photographer was much different. He was far more friendly and encouraging. I saw another side of Mrs. A too. She stripped down to her skimpy blouse and skirt and put on an overall like a tea lady and some flat shoes, which she must have brought for the purpose. She was prepared to work tirelessly all day as my 'dresser'.

First she substantially increased my make-up for the studio lights. This involved much heavier application of rouge and lipstick than would be worn outside or even for evening wear. She obviously knew about these things having been a photographic fashion model herself.

I had previously thought of professional photography being a sort of 'watch-the-birdie' affair with the photographer under a black cover and some bright flash with smoke. I was surprised to see it was done with a modern camera which the photographer had on a strap round his neck. He didn't even use a flash.

He was more like a seaside promenade photographer taking snaps. In fact he was so fast with taking the pictures and winding on the film that I was not sure exactly when he was actually taking a picture. This took the pressure off me and enabled me to relax and just follow his instructions.

The surprising thing was how he talked to me while he was photographing me. Instead of my standing still in a pose waiting to be photographed, he asked me to move. He showed me a walkway in the studio that kept me in the lights but where I could walk up and down and turn in a normal relaxed way.

I found this much easier than adopting a fixed pose, since it was just what I had done in Mrs. Atkinson's hallway. I strutted and swayed my false hips and turned rapidly so the coat would swirl around behind me. Paul, the photographer, would follow me, snapping away. He would give me instructions such as, turn left, twist your hips to the right, look over your left shoulder.

He even got me to do complete turns which fortunately Glynis had taught me to do as part of my deportment training. I didn't need my restrictive slip any more to take small lady-like steps. I found myself moving gracefully and effortlessly even when wearing my highest heels.

In the studio there were a number of props. One was a stool and the other was a railing. Paul had me sitting on the stool and leaning back on the railing. All the time he was talking to me, encouraging and praising me for doing it so well. I really felt it was rather like were dancing together. I enjoyed this closeness, as if we were feeding off each other.

What I hadn't expected was the heat of the lights. Naturally the coat would heat up after a while, especially if it was buttoned up to the chin against the imaginary rain. When Paul called out 'Change', Glynis would appear to release me from my rubber encasement. She deftly undid the buttons which I could not because of my gloves. She handed me a towel to pat off any perspiration on my skin.

I was only wearing my underwear so there was nothing to ruche up and show under the raincoat. So when Glynis held out the next coat to put on, there was a wonderful cold sensation on my shoulders, midriff and the tops of my thighs. A shiver of chill and pleasure went through me as Glynis buttoned me up and arranged the coat or cape to look its best. She would do a final inspection of my make-up and maybe put on a bit more powder. She then turned me round and pushed me gently back into the lights and towards Paul.

I felt as if I was in a dream being bounced between these two lovely people who were both controlling me in this dream of femininity. Sadly all too soon Glynis announced that this was to be the last shot.

As in any fashion show, there are some garments which are not expected to sell but are there to provide extravagant glamour and style to the range. This last item was a snow-white rubberised cape with a black mandarin collar and black buttons. Glynis put it around my shoulders and I had a blissful moment to enjoy the cool fabric against my skin. Then she pulled off my everyday gloves and pulled on a pair of long black rubberised gloves that came up above my elbows. They were elasticated at the top and were pulled into shape at my wrist by a series of small buttons.

"You see, I remembered," said Glynis, as she did up the buttons. I was imprisoned in the gloves which I could not have undone myself. However no thought of escape crossed my mind.

"Bend forward," she said, and put a small black pillbox hat on my head. Then she did up the small black buttons of the cape, right up to the chin. I remember the collar had a soft velvety feel against my neck.

"Arms out," she said and I slid my gloved hands out through two small slits. These only allowed me to get my wrists and forearms out and stopped me at the elbow.

"Don't raise your elbows, you will spoil the shape." she said.

Into my hands she put an absurdly small umbrella with a long handle. Clearly the umbrella would not provide any significant protection from the weather but it was a very elegant prop for such a flamboyant garment.

Once back in the lights and under Paul's instructions, I felt I was walking on air. The cape was so responsive to my movements that it seemed to slide over my shoulders as I turned. The folds of the cape followed my movements and caressed my thighs. One thing about a rain cape is that it does not get as hot as a raincoat. The air inside has much more room to circulate and the movements move the air around and push it out through the arm slits.

I twisted and flounced; I smiled and I pouted, I felt that everything moved with me as in an elegant dance. I played with the umbrella, opening and shutting it, hiding behind it or looking coyly over the top of it. I even lifted my elbows but only when Paul told me to as part of his choreography. I was sure the cape would still have a glamorous shape.

Finally it was over. All the coats and capes were back on their hangers and the lights were turned off. I put my dress back on and was sent to the ladies' to take off my stage make-up and put on my normal level of daytime make-up.

Then we had to pack the raincoats and rain capes

back into their individually labelled boxes and stack them near the door ready for collection. I took particular care in the folding and wrapping of the magnificent white rain cape that I had so recently been wearing.

On the way out we said goodbye to Paul who was getting his films ready to take to the developers. He gave me a kiss on the cheek and said he would be happy for me to come and model for him again.

"I think we deserve a cup of tea and a piece of cake," said Glynis as we stood on the pavement outside the studio. She was restored to her former glory in her mauve costume suit, high heels and fur stole. I was restored to my schoolgirl drabness.

I looked round for somewhere but the part of Manchester we were in looked unpromising.

"Not here," Glynis said. "After your performance today, we deserve nothing less than the Midland!"

So we trotted across Manchester to the Midland for tea. Once we got in there we both realised how much the day had taken out of us and how tired we were. Nevertheless I still found the experience daunting. This was not a glorified pub called an hotel in Perston but Manchester's premier hotel. Glynis told me it was at this hotel that Mr. Rolls and Mr. Royce had first met to discuss setting up a company to produce motor cars.

The toilets were palatial and fortunately Glynis came with me to show me how to behave in such splendor. However we were both too tired to really relish the occasion.

"I think it is early to bed again tonight," said Glynis, "but we must come again and next time we must dress you in something more pretty."

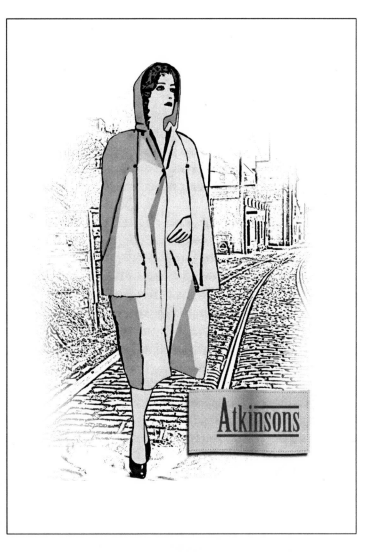

15

The Holiday

A few days later Paul came to the house to show us the rush prints of the photographs. I was amazed how many there were. He somehow had time to change films because some were black and white and some were colour. They all looked the same to me at first, apart from the colours of the coats themselves.

Slowly Glynis and Paul selected those that would become the base for the new catalogue. Unfortunately, this being the early days of colour photography, some had not come out the right colour. The best of these would have to be doctored to get back to the correct colour.

It would take several weeks of work to get sets of the selected photographs ready to send out to the representatives. We all worked hard and finally we were ready to launch the new range.

The next stage was to take the show on the road. In the fashion world the seasons are reversed. The time to be selling a new autumn range of rainwear is the previous spring and the selling season starts immediately after New Year.

There were big trade fairs in London and Harrogate where all the fashion houses exhibited their ranges to fashion buyers of department stores and the few clothing chains that existed then. Then there were regional shows for the buyers of the many independent clothing stores. In some cases we put on our own shows for special customers who could be expected to place large orders.

I was the dumb model while Mrs. Atkinson did all the talking, charming and negotiating. We took no one from the factory as they would probably have recognised me. Sometimes we had help from our local representatives but they didn't know me from Adam, or Eve!

When we had to stay away in hotels, Mrs. Atkinson booked us a twin bedded room. This was not just to save money but also she knew where I was. Sometimes she would stay down in the bar talking with our representatives or buyers. However she always insisted that I go up to the room immediately after we had eaten, giving the reason to anyone who was with us that I was tired or had a headache. I realise now she was protecting me, not so much from discovery, but from some of the men on the buying circuit who had a strong predatory instinct. I had instructions to lock the door and not to let anyone in but her.

Eventually it was all over and we had a very good harvest of provisional and promised orders. These would be confirmed in the spring and then made up during the summer for delivery in the early autumn.

Mrs. A decided it was time to take a holiday. She asked my mother for permission to take me on holiday with her to France.

I was both shocked and excited at the prospect. I had never been abroad before and of course did not have a passport. As always Mrs. A used her ingenuity to get things to happen. She got Paul to take some suitably androgynous photos of me with my long hair pulled back and out of sight. Then she got a JP friend of hers to sign that they were a true likeness of me.

Although the passport would be in my male name, Mrs. A made it clear I was going on holiday with her 'as Joanna'. She said we would only need to show the passport at Dover and Calais and they wouldn't look that closely. It would be tidier and so much more economical she said. Once again I had to trust her.

We had already started going to the theatre and on

other outings together, with me as Joanna, and nothing had gone awry. I felt so much like a girl when I was out with her that I never thought I could be anything else.

We went into Manchester on several shopping expeditions to buy clothes for our holiday. She bought me a couple of simple floral dresses and a pair of low-heeled white wedge-heel sandals. For herself she didn't buy much. Mrs. A said she would be able to get a much better choice of clothes in Paris.

It emerged that Paris was only to be our first staging post. Our ultimate destination was to be the Côte d'Azur (Coast of Blue) or playground of the rich. Mrs. A had not been to the South of France since before the war and hoped that it would by now have regained its pre-war glory.

Finally the day of our departure arrived. I had one suitcase but Glynis had three. It did not dawn on me until later what was the real purpose of this trip. Glynis wanted to re-launch herself in France and cultivate her circle of friends in Paris. Her grandparents, with whom she used to live as a girl, had left Paris at the time of the German invasion and had died during the time of the occupation.

We travelled first from Central Station in Manchester to London. In those days the journey took most of the day. The weather was the usual Manchester gloom so we both wore our raincoats. Mrs. A wore her emerald green raincoat with the loose back. It had a belt which did up at the front but left the back loose. This had the practical benefit of keeping her cool even when it was muggy.

My old serviceable navy blue rubberised raincoat had been replaced for the holiday with a new larger and longer one to accommodate my recent growth. Thanks to my better diet and lifestyle, I was now filling out. I was less painfully thin and a little broader across the shoulders. Nonetheless there was nothing glamorous about this coat. It was navy blue, came halfway down my calves and had a sturdy belt to cinch in my waist. However, the pristine rubberised inside had a lovely feel to it. I felt more feminine in it than in my old one, which barely fitted me now.

Mrs. A said she thought it better if I looked as much like a schoolgirl or a trainee nun as possible to avoid 'the wrong sort of attention'. I only had a vague idea what she meant but thought there was more to it than my true gender being discovered. I realise now that there was a second reason for this decision. Probably she felt at a subconscious level that she did not want any competition. Such is the insecurity of beautiful women when they get to a certain age!

When we finally arrived at Euston, Glynis had all our cases put into a taxi and we went to a small hotel she knew near Victoria. The hotel was austere and the food was awful. Nevertheless we made the best of it and at 9.30 the next morning we were walking down the platform at Victoria Station towards an impressive gate with an arch over it. As we approached the arch I could read the words 'Golden Arrow – Fleche d'Or'. We were booked on the 10.00am boat train to Paris!

This was a different kind of train travel than the grimy British Railways that was the norm in the 1950s. It was a 'Pullman' service with big comfortable seats and waiter service. What is more the train left on the dot of 10 o'clock.

We drank our coffee and watched the Kent countryside flash by. Mrs. A said it would be safer not to eat anything yet because of the possibility of sea-sickness. The weather was overcast and windy.

Once again I was impressed at the difference between the toilets in these carriages and those on ordinary trains. We even agreed to give up our precious raincoats which were taken from us by an official and hung up for us in a cloakroom nearby.

We needed our coats for the channel crossing. The sea of the English Channel seemed so much more real than the sea I remember from Blackpool or Southport. After the ship pulled out from the shelter of the harbour, we hit the real swell of the waves. Mrs. A was of course a good sailor but I didn't know if I would be affected by the sea-sickness that she had warned me about.

Mrs. A sat inside reading but I chose to spend most of the time out on the deck watching the white cliffs get smaller as we headed out for France. This was an exhilarating experience, especially wrapped up securely in my new long raincoat. As taught by Glynis, I only wore a light blouse under my coat. I could feel the spray and spots of rain hitting me as I walked around the deck but felt safe and protected. It was great fun to feel my hood flapping against the sides of my face. I also enjoyed the feeling through my thin stockings of the skirt of my coat being blown around my legs. The hood was tightly tied under my chin so it could not be blown down but nevertheless the wind had a good try.

I found a position on the deck where I could hold on tight to the railing and feel the wind, rain and spray buffeting me. It was a wonderful experience. For the first time, it seemed, I had time to think about my situation. I considered what a wonderful turn my life had taken since I had first walked in through the gates at Atkinson's, nearly three years before.

I could not have imagined how my dreams would be developed and fulfilled by Mrs. A. I thought of my school mates. As far as I knew they had moved on to the predictable humdrum jobs of a northern industrial town. They would have no more idea of going to France than learning to fly. But on top of that they could not conceive of the world that I was experiencing with Mrs. Atkinson. I just stood there and let the feelings of wonder and gratitude wash over me.

It seemed to take a lot longer to get to France than

to leave England. Very slowly the boat came along the French coast and finally into the harbour at Calais. I was desperate to see something of France and to see how different it was from England.

The first thing to strike me was how well Glynis spoke French to the porters who brought our luggage into the customs shed. The formalities were quickly over and we were now in a smooth-running electric train powered by overhead cables. This was not a Pullman train and it didn't need to be. French trains were run to a much better standard. I sat in my comfortable window seat and looked out into the fading light to see what I could of the French countryside.

We were in Paris within a couple of hours and then my real exposure to France began. We were booked into a small hotel near the Gare du Nord so that the porters could carry our luggage to it, for an extra tip. I thought we would eat in the hotel. Not at all! Mrs. A had a whole list of arrangements made to meet up with her pre-war friends in Paris. We started that evening with dinner with an old girlfriend.

Mrs. A had started to teach me French back in England and had obtained some basic textbooks for me. However I could not understand the gabble as she caught up with her many friends in Paris. She introduced me to them briefly. She had taught me what to say in French to make the right initial impression. After that I just had to sit and look interested.

After I told Mrs. A I felt stupid not being able to understand, she let me take my dictionary and notebook with me and told me to make a list of words I heard and look them up. She would then go through the list afterwards and have a conversation with me in French using the words. She was a brilliant tutor and after a few days refused to speak to me in English. As a result my French came on in leaps and bounds.

I remember that several things made a major impact on me. First we had left dreary Lancashire in what seemed like the depths of winter and in Paris it was spring! The leaves were out, there were flowers everywhere and the weather was warm.

Second, the women were magnificently dressed. I could see now why Glynis had decided to buy her clothes in Paris. She took me to the 'big stores' as well as the small boutiques and even asked for my advice on her purchases.

Then there was the food! Glynis had introduced me to better food in England but we were still limited in our choices. Rationing had only recently ended. Anyway garlic was not readily available in Brunley. Everything that was put before me tasted so different and so good!

We spent several days in Paris, partly shopping for Glynis and also visiting her friends and old work colleagues. There was little time for visiting traditional tourist attractions but we did manage a quick visit to the Louvre and Glynis gave me a brief introduction to French history from sights we saw through the windows of taxis.

Then we were on the train again, heading for the French Riviera! If it had been spring in Paris, it seemed that in Nice it was summer. Here we did not have much visiting to do as Glynis didn't know many people. So I had much more of her attention.

She became quite confiding and told me quite a few things about her early life that I didn't know. The most significant was that soon after returning from France to marry Mr. Atkinson (junior), she had had a daughter. It had been a difficult birth and sadly the little girl had only lived for a few months. From what I gathered she had been told by her doctors that she could not have more children and had become very depressed. Mr. Atkinson had taken her to France to help her recover and she took up her career of modeling and designing again in Paris. As a result she and her husband had spent more time in France than in England. Fortunately the Atkinson business enabled them to live the good life of the rich between Paris and the Riviera.

The prospect of war had brought them back to England and it seemed they had put their luxury lifestyle behind them to devote themselves to the military preparations which were then under way.

The war and subsequent events meant that this was the first real holiday that Glynis had had for many years. Now that she had got back a taste for the good life, she was certainly going to enjoy it.

With this more relaxed relationship, I plucked up the courage to ask her what she meant by 'the wrong sort of attention'. At first she was a little flustered but being the strong character she was, she came back with a proposal.

"All right, if you want to know, this evening you will find out."

That evening she dressed me in one of the glamorous dresses she had bought in Paris and lent me a pair of her high heeled sandals. She did my make-up as only she could and let me wear my hair down. She lent me some jewellery and put some of her scent on me.

That night in the restaurant we were mobbed by men coming up to introduce themselves and ask if we had everything we needed. We had always had some attention from men but they were usually older and exclusively interested in Glynis. Now they came in all shapes, sizes and nationalities. They were giving us at least equal attention.

It was very flattering and they were very charming. I could just about understand what they were saying but my French was not good enough to reply in an appropriate way. Fortunately Glynis was adept in putting them off in a charming way and knowing when and how much to accept their hospitality.

We had so much fun avoiding the wrong men and discussing the merits of the nice ones that it became a regular occurrence for Glynis to 'glam me up' in the evenings.

We must have got ourselves quite a reputation, as we clicked and tinkled along the promenade arm-in-arm in our high heels, glittering dresses and jangling jewellery, on our way between our restaurant of the evening and the casino. The journey home was even noisier as by then we were usually both quite tipsy. We were not so much clicking and jingling so much as clattering and giggling uncontrollably as we supported each other back to our hotel.

On one day a spring storm blew in from the Mediterranean. It was raining as we got up and Glynis was pleased that we would have an opportunity to wear our raincoats as we had taken the trouble to bring them all this way.

We had become rather like giddy schoolgirls. We decided to only wear our skimpy sunbathing clothes underneath so there was plenty of bare flesh to be in contact with the smooth rubberised surfaces inside.

I didn't wear the belt on mine so it hung loose from the shoulders and would be cooler. Glynis agreed that this seemed to be a much more stylish and appropriate way to wear it in France. It meant when I turned the whole coat moved behind me and slithered against my bare legs. We spent the day swishing around the shops and cafes of the town in our raincoats.

In those days in France, double rooms also meant double beds. Glynis didn't seem to think anything about sharing a bed with me. Fortunately the beds were quite big so I was able to lie close to my side without any danger of inadvertently touching Glynis.

My hair removal programme needed to continue because the rogue hairs were more conspicuous in the bright

Mediterranean sunshine.

We didn't have the usual rain cape with us of course. We didn't even have a suitable chair. We had to use the dressing table stool and Mrs. A improvised with my raincoat. She put it on me back-to-front and used the cuff straps to secure my arms behind my back. Then she used the belt around my knees to give herself a secure place to sit.

One evening, because of the warm balmy air, Glynis was just wearing her underwear. We started in the usual way but the beautiful setting sun, the cool sea breeze blowing the net curtains, and the wine we had had at lunchtime, must have combined to make Glynis particularly relaxed and playful.

As usual I got excited at her proximity and my penis was very obviously stretching the fabric of my raincoat. Maybe she could see the admiration in my eyes and she became increasingly amorous and excited. I could feel that she was definitely pushing up against my erect penis and closing her eyes, which meant she couldn't have been looking for hairs.

Then she stood up and in a low husky whisper said, "Stand up Joanna."

With some timidity I did so, wondering if I had done something to upset her.

She put one hand on my arm to steady me and with the other hand gently pushed me backwards. With my knees strapped together I could only shuffle backwards with very small steps but I knew we were moving towards the bed.

Then with a final shove, she pushed me backwards onto the bed. The next moment she jumped on top of me and started kissing me. She lay with her thighs astride my legs and rubbed her belly on mine. She pushed her warm crotch against my erect penis which was of course imprisoned inside my raincoat but straining against the rubberised fabric to get upright.

I always knew she was beautiful but in the full flood of her sexual desire and excitement she was transformed to transcendent beauty. What shocked me was how noisy she was prepared to be even though the hotel room had double doors. So pent-up and consuming were her emotions that she was sobbing as she consumed my face with greedy kisses.

I could only lie there with my arms pinned behind me and my knees locked together in my rapidly heating up raincoat. However I was glad of its protection because I could feel her fingernails scratching against it down my arms and up my thighs.

I realise I must have provided exactly the right shape for her to ride herself to the inevitable climax which seemed of earth-shattering proportions. Once she calmed down a bit, she changed her position slightly. She brought her legs together on top of me with my erect penis between them. Then she moved her hips gently to massage my penis with her thighs.

The feeling was exquisite and very soon after that my world exploded with a combination of sensations which rocked me to my foundations and caused me to burst out with sobs of my own. I didn't know where I was and seemed to be falling backwards into a bottomless pit. I forgot the strain on my arms and the sweltering heat of my rubber prison.

Later, much later, I woke up to find Glynis lying on her side with her head on her hand looking into my face with an expression of quiet satisfaction.

"Well, well, well," was all she could say as she rolled me over to release my wrists.

Glynis had to wrap towels around my legs to soak up some of the perspiration which poured from me as I shuffled to the bathroom. There she released me from my rubber raincoat, from which cascaded perspiration all over the bathroom floor.

Glynis filled the bath and we both tumbled into it. We washed and dried each other and then fell back into bed. There was no restaurant or casino that evening!

The rest of the holiday flew by. Our days followed a regular routine. We spent the mornings on the terrace or in the shops, had lunch and retired to bed to make love. We had afternoon tea on our balcony before dressing elaborately for the evening. After dinner we did a quick tour of the bars and the casino, clattering on our high heels and politely evading the attention of admirers. We did not stay out late. We were in bed early so we could spend long nights making love. Once the gates to her emotions had been opened, Glynis had a lot of catching up to do.

A set of enlarged colour illustrations may be downloaded from
www.dominantdesigns.co.uk   or
email: **pictures@dominantdesigns.co.uk**

16

The Homecoming

The day for our return arrived all too quickly. We travelled up to Paris during the day and then took the night boat train to London. The benefit of this method of travel was that the sleeper carriages were transported onto the boat and made the journey all the way to London. This was intended to provide an uninterrupted night's sleep.

In our case we both slept badly and were aware of every stop and start and every strange movement that our carriage made. The crossing was smooth but we arrived in Victoria station tired and irritable in the early hours of the morning.

We both knew that things could not go on as they had before and some difficult decisions would have to be made. There was no question in my mind that I loved Glynis and wanted to stay with her on whatever basis we could manage. She on her side was much more in control of her feelings and much more of a realist about the practicalities of life. She was not prepared to talk about the future on the journey but I could tell she was thinking about it.

The journey from Euston to Manchester on British Railways seemed to take forever. The future seemed to me to get bleaker the closer we came to home. Little did I know that matters would be taken out of our hands by two significant events!

The first of these hit us as soon as we got back to Brunley. Mrs. Atkinson Senior had finally died. She had become a victim of what we would now call senile dementia. She hadn't been able to recognise Glynis or anyone else for about the previous 6 months. Glynis had reduced her visits to once a week, although she had said even these were pointless.

It was most unfortunate that the death occurred while Glynis was out of the country. This meant that other members of the family had to be brought in to handle the formalities and start the funeral arrangements. Then the questions and rumours started. Where was Glynis and who was she with? The staff in the office knew the name of the hotel we were staying at and they did send a telegram. However it must have arrived just after we had left.

When the will was read it became apparent that old Mr. Atkinson had done a deal with Glynis. It seems that when he became ill following the death of his two sons, he had agreed with Glynis that she would run the business after his death and look after Mrs. Atkinson Senior during the remainder of her life. Thereafter the majority shareholding in the company would pass to her.

The relatives were furious. Like all hangers-on, they were happy to let Glynis do the work of running the business which provided them with some income and perks. However as she was only a family member by marriage, they felt she should not be given the family home and total control of the future of the business.

This was the beginning of bad feelings which quickly became a battle. All sorts of grievances and rumours were fed into the feud. This included her holidaying in France while Mrs. A Senior was dying, and her promoting a warehouse boy into a position of authority, and then taking him to live at the family home. Then there was the appearance of this mysterious niece who was used as a photographic model in preference to other family members.

The relatives became aggressive and involved lawyers. Glynis had to do the same to defend herself.

As soon as she got to know about Mrs. Atkinson

Senior, on the day we had arrived back, Glynis packed me off home. She knew she would have to accommodate at the house the relatives who would come for the funeral. She told me to go and have my hair cut and then go to the office and make myself useful.

I was glad to get back to work because it was somewhere to go and occupy myself. I was suffering from severe shock. Everything seemed unreal. In a matter of days I had gone from sharing a luxury hotel bedroom on the French Riviera with a beautiful woman to sharing a small bedroom in Brunley with my two younger brothers.

Because of the funeral and related activities, I was unable to talk to Glynis for about two weeks. She had sent me a note saying because of the funeral and visitors it would be best not to contact her until after they had all gone and she gave the date on which I should telephone her in the evening.

The second event was that during the time I was at home waiting to get back in touch with Glynis, I received an envelope headed 'On Her Majesty's Service'. In it was a letter informing me that I was to be 'called up' for my National Service and was to report to the Caterick military camp on a date set in four months' time.

This was a devastating blow. I had thought because I had rheumatic fever as a child, I would be exempt. I went to see my doctor and he said they no longer regarded that as an automatic reason for exemption. He said I would be given a full medical but based on my current state of health, he could see no reason why I would be turned down.

On the designated evening for ringing Glynis, I read her the letter over the phone. There was a long silence. I think she was crying. Finally she told me in a choking voice to telephone her the next evening, and put down the phone.

The next evening when I telephoned she was composed and even a little cold. She told me to collect together all the figures and information to brief her on what had happened in the business in the period since we had left. She told me to come to her house with everything at 2pm on Saturday.

That meant even more days of impatient waiting to see Glynis. At least I was able make myself busy doing something that would be of help to her. Finally Saturday arrived and I trudged up the hill with the papers she wanted, and my call-up letter.

She greeted me formally. This immediately confirmed that I had to proceed very carefully. I decided to keep quiet and let her do the talking. She was dressed in a smart black suit and low-heeled black shoes. She had her hair tied back and was wearing simple but thick make-up. She looked tired and strained. All signs of her holiday had gone from her face. I even thought I saw signs of puffiness around the eyes which would indicate she had been crying.

She had assumed the air of authority that went with her job again. She addressed me as John in the way she had when I had first worked for her and long before Joanna was born. I knew that she was Mrs. Atkinson again and that was what I should call her.

I on my side felt the old days had gone. I sat there uncomfortably with my badly cut short hair, in a rough-collared shirt, heavy male shoes and hairy sports jacket. All my soft femininity and neatness had drained away.

Mrs. Atkinson didn't even offer me a cup of tea. She took me into the rather cold front room which I had never been in before. We sat at a small table. She asked me to show her the figures and start my report immediately. She listened carefully and asked a few questions.

Once she had got the overall position clear in her mind, she started to lose interest. Eventually she pushed the papers to one side.

"Now we need to talk about the future and I need to

tell you a few things," she said, turning towards me. The strain in her face was now very obvious.

She explained some of the difficulties she was having with the Atkinson family.

"I don't know how it will develop," she said. "My solicitor says that I have the law on my side and they do not have a case. However they can make trouble and create bad feelings among the staff."

"They don't begin to appreciate all that I have done in building up the business. As long as they get their payments for doing nothing, they couldn't care less. I have slaved over this business for ten years since dear old Tom Atkinson died, and they didn't lift a finger to help me look after Elsie Atkinson for all those years."

She was starting to show some emotion. I realised that if she had been crying, it was more likely to be tears of anger at the developing situation than about me.

"I ask myself, what am I doing in this godforsaken town? Am I here to support that group of bloodsuckers? Do they think I will spend the rest of my life supporting them?"

"Well they can think again. I can sell the business and this house and live comfortably for the rest of my life in France," she said defiantly.

I sat still, listening and nodding. I hoped that listening silently was helpful.

"I could live and work in France again. I have dual nationality, you know, and the weather would be a damn sight better than here."

She went on for some time. Then she took me into the kitchen and made us some tea. I could see that the return of the volatile French side of her character had survived from her holiday. Nevertheless she relied on English tea for her consolation.

Once she had calmed down, she became warmer towards me. Now she sat opposite me across the kitchen table. I was pleased that she was now more friendly but I had a presentiment about what was to come.

"So we should talk about us," she said at last. Once again I knew Mrs. Atkinson well enough to know this meant she would talk and I would listen.

"We had a wonderful holiday in France but that was what it was – a holiday. I am very fond of you both as John and Joanna, but we must be realistic. By the time you are my age, I will be an old hag!"

She said the words 'old hag' with Gallic panache, but nonetheless she meant them. I tried to protest but she brushed my words aside.

"You are a very clever boy. You can have a brilliant career. You will find a beautiful English girl who will suit you much better than a neurotic French woman twice your age. I can find one of those penniless aristocrats we met in the South of France to keep me company, and make his life a misery."

Once again she held up her hand as I tried to disagree.

"You will have lots of beautiful children which I cannot give you."

Once again I tried to tell her none of that mattered. She stood up.

"Listen John, you have a choice. Either, you accept my decision and we can be friends until it is time for you to go away, or ..." there was a slight hesitation and I thought a slight quiver of her lip. "... not come to this house again."

There may have been a brief quiver of her lip but I could tell by the expression in her eyes that she meant it. I put my elbows on the kitchen table and my head in my hands. Of course she was right but at that age I didn't think I could live without her. Nevertheless I lifted my head and looked at her as she stood there waiting.

"I accept," I said slightly melodramatically.

"Good," she said and sat down again.

"Now, we must make some plans. What date do you have to report for your Military service?"

I told her and she started to work out how many weeks away that was.

"On Monday morning we both start back at work in earnest. I would like your help to get the business into the best shape we can so we can get a very good price if I decide to sell.

"We will need to chase up the orders for next autumn based on the new range and get the orders into production. We can also make some extra stock which will go into the valuation at full wholesale price. I have been recommended to use a specialist firm of accountants in Manchester who will put every penny of value we can come up with into the asking price."

I began to pity the people who would be up against her when it came to a valuation of the company and negotiating a purchase price for it. She had a very shrewd business head.

Since we came back from our holiday, I had begun to see her as a quintessential French business woman. I had met some while we were in Paris and could tell they were as hard as nails and very good negotiators. I could foresee that she would have a string of potential purchasers and she would be playing them off against each other.

"Then we must make some preparations for you. I have spoken to a senior military man I know and asked his advice."

I expressed surprise that she knew such a person.

"When you are a woman on your own, you need to cultivate influential friends and allies. You never know when you might need them. He says that the best way to take advantage of this situation is for you to sign up for a three- or five-year period. The army will then educate and train you to a very high standard and you might become an officer."

Mrs. Atkinson said she had told him how well I had done and that I had passed all my exams at the local college. He had said he would be willing to meet me so he could form some impression of me and maybe put in a good word for me. I was flabbergasted and it must have shown. She laughed.

"You still have a lot to learn about the way the world really works and how you make progress in it."

Then she suggested we should go to the pictures. I was so pleased that we were on at least familiar terms again that I immediately agreed. She looked in the evening paper. She didn't think it was a good idea to go out together in Brunley or anywhere else where we might be recognised.

She made us some sandwiches and then went upstairs to get ready. She came down looking like the most glamorous woman I would ever want to be seen with. She had put up her hair and wore a dark full skirt and a trim tight-fitting blouse.

"The weather looks quite threatening so I am going to wear a raincoat. Which one would you like me to wear?"

I chose the long green one with the loose back that she had worn to go on holiday.

"Well, I can put on my higher heels to wear with that coat. Would you like that?" she said.

"It is a good job you have grown otherwise I would have been taller than you."

She chose a romantic weepy film. I can't remember much about it except that we both cried. It must have been the relief of having reached a new kind of relationship. We had to share my hankie and fortunately it was clean.

On the way back to the car, she linked my arm in hers, in a way which was playful and girlish. I felt so proud I thought my heart would burst.

17

The Last Chapter

In the weeks that followed we were both very busy. It was obvious to both of us that the business had lost some momentum during the time we had been away on holiday and the time taken up by the funeral of Mrs. Atkinson Senior.

Now was the key time for finalising orders for delivery by the autumn. Mrs. A was back in the office everyday and spent much of her time on the telephone chasing up and clinching orders from her best customers. Her activity substantially increased the levels of orders for the new range. I on my side had to plan the orders for fabric and other requirements for production to meet the orders.

The timing worked well because I had to report for my National Service in mid-September, by which time all these orders would have been delivered. This would be the ideal time to sell the business as a record profit was in prospect. Of course no one at the factory or in the Atkinson family knew of the grand plan.

I wasn't kept informed of the maneuvering with the family obstructers. It may have been that they had cooled down. However once Mrs. A had decided she wanted to shake the dust of Brunley from her feet, there was no going back.

We were often both the last people to leave the factory in the evening.

"You know John," said Mrs. Atkinson one evening, "I have never heard any whisper that anyone here has guessed who was modeling our raincoats and capes in our new catalogue and at the trade shows. That is in part a credit to Paul's photography and to your hard work and discretion."

I was very flattered and very pleased that she had pulled off this plan.

Despite being so busy, Mrs. A still made time available to prepare me for my coming ordeal. One Saturday afternoon we went deep into Cheshire in her car to meet the high-ranking military man.

We arrived at a large house set in its own grounds. When we arrived we were greeted by a middle-aged man who was tying up some plants in the garden. He was wearing baggy trousers and a cardigan. I thought he must be the gardener. In my innocence I assumed the military man would be wearing uniform. At the time I knew nothing of military ranks so when he was introduced to me as Major General Suchabody, the title meant nothing to me. Later I learned that he was not even retired but still working part-time at the War Office, and thus was extremely high–ranking and influential.

"Come in and have some tea," he said, in a way that expected no discussion.

He was obviously very warm towards Mrs. Atkinson and it became apparent that he had known her husband too. To my surprise he was also very friendly to me and interested to know what I had done so far. He wanted to know about my father's fate but I could tell him very little. I told him I could find out from my mother.

"Too many young men these days see National Service as something to be got through with minimum disruption to their lives. For someone like you it can be a great opportunity. There isn't much real fighting to be done these days. We don't need more warriors; we need more men who can get on with and influence all sorts of people, inside and outside the military. These days we are more concerned with winning hearts and minds than winning battles. A young man like you could do very well. The trick is to play the system. Volunteer for anything that is going and make sure you persuade the right people to be interested in your progress."

I didn't realise it at the time but it was one of the best pieces of advice of my life.

Mrs. Atkinson also took a hand in my broader education. She started me reading serious newspapers and reading biographies of military men and anything else she could find about the army.

She took me to a good barber in Manchester and he taught me how someone who was going up in the world should have their hair styled. She took me to a good Gents Outfitter and bought me a new wardrobe of clothes for my new life. I offered to pay towards them but she would hear nothing of it. Her faith in my potential career was very encouraging.

After our momentous Saturday afternoon, when we had decided on the fate of both our lives, Mrs. Atkinson took my education in another direction. We went out frequently together and she taught me how to woo women.

"You remember those charming men we met in France?" she said. "Most of them were over forty but if you can learn to be as charming as them before you are twenty, you can be irresistible and win the heart of any woman you choose."

She set up my individual charm school. Maybe she enjoyed the attention I lavished on her as part of my training. I certainly enjoyed any opportunity to be with her on familiar terms.

We went to concerts, theatre and the races. She found a military tattoo for us to go to. She even let me escort her to some formal social occasions for which I had to hire evening dress. She introduced me as her nephew and she assured people that I was on the way to having a brilliant military career.

All this had the function of removing the fear of meeting and talking with people who I might have considered had higher social standing. I may still have had the remains of a Brunley accent but I was not willing to be intimidated by that.

She said that once I got into the military I would have plenty of opportunity to seek the company of better educated and better spoken people than me. Mingling with them would soon rub off on me.

Looking back on my successful military career, I can only say she was right. Because I had learned to win the friendship and cooperation of anyone I encountered, I rapidly found my way into better company.

She must have blessed me in some way because her high ambitions for me actually did come true. Almost certainly the reference she provided for me, and the endorsement from the senior military man, played their part at the beginning.

Even the nice English girl came along and I managed to get her interest to the point of love and marriage. And yes we have some very fine children. Again I must thank Mrs. Atkinson for that too.

As the time for me to leave Brunley approached, I asked if we could write to each other. She seemed unwilling to agree. She said she didn't know where she would be and it could be difficult. In the end she said she would keep in touch through my mother.

She didn't expect to be in Brunley for much longer. She said on one occasion that if I wanted to take any souvenirs of my time with Atkinson's, now was the time to do it. She gave me the raincoat that had been silver when I first saw her wearing it. Although it had lost its shine and become grey, for me it was still a reminder of the impact of my first meeting with her. She also gave me the long blue raincoat I had worn to go to France.

In addition she let me choose some of the original pictures from the wonderful photo shoot. I kept these with the raincoats in a suitcase of old clothes which I left at my mother's house. I did not go back to Brunley for some years and sadly the suitcase and all its contents were mislaid when my mother moved. So now all I have are the memories.

I had thought my maturing into manhood and a happy marriage would put all my boyhood desires and interests behind me. However in recent years I have found the memories of those giddy days coming back to me more and more. Maybe that is why I have willingly made the effort to tell this story.

I realise that those events were particular to that time cannot be recreated. A visit to the derelict remains of the Atkinson factory and warehouse was a sad confirmation of that fact. However I sometimes wonder how young people today with my predilections, and I am sure they exist, indulge and even fulfill their fantasies.

My brief excursions into pornography have been disappointing. I can imagine Mrs Atkinson's horror at their vulgarity. I am sure there must be a better way!

***

The day finally came for me to go. I was due to leave from Exchange Station quite early in the morning and it was agreed that Mrs. A would pick me up at my mother's house and take me down to Manchester.

I had worked out by now the basis of the relationship between Mrs. A and my mother. Having been school friends they still had a strong affinity even though their lives had taken such different paths.

After my mother had been widowed, Mrs. A had been anxious to help. My mother would never have accepted charity but once I had started work at Atkinson's, Glynis could justify making various extra payments because of the extra work I was doing for the company. Thus my official pay did not go up much but the difference was paid to my mother to help with the costs of bringing up the younger children. So it was that my mother was anxious I should work hard and do whatever Mrs. A asked to justify the trust she was putting in me.

On the journey down to Manchester, I tried to thank Mrs. A for all the help she had been to our family. All she said was she would appreciate it if nobody else knew about it.

I also tried to thank her for all the help she had given me in my education, both formal and in life. She was more gracious and said it was a pleasure.

"If there is one thing I hope you have learned," she said after a while and then paused, "it is to be strong enough to say no to yourself, when it is the right thing to do!"

I didn't know for sure if that related to our decision about us but I thought it would be wise to say I hoped so too.

When we arrived at Exchange Station we found we had time to spare because the train was late coming in. So we sat in the British Railways cafeteria, endlessly stirring our abominable coffee and fiddling with the sugar lumps. All we could find to say to each other were banalities.

When it was time to go, I picked up my suitcase and newspaper. I moved slowly towards the barrier and she walked silently by my side. When we were still some way from the crowd of people at the barrier she stopped.

"John, this is as far as I can come," she said in a slightly strangled voice.

She turned towards me and before I could put down my case, she grabbed both my arms and held them to my sides. Then she rose on her toes to kiss me on both cheeks in the French way.

"*Adieu Cheri et merci,*" she said and gave me a warm

smile.

Then she turned and I watched her walk away. She was wearing a neat brimmed hat and her emerald green raincoat which she wore fully belted in a businesslike way. Nevertheless she looked to me just like the romantic heroine from one of the 40s films she loved so much.

Even though she was obviously as upset as I was, she still walked with her shoulders straight and her usual slight swing of the hips, which I would now call her Gallic swagger. She had an air of defiance about her and I knew that whatever developed at Atkinson's, she would come out on top.

I watched her walk across the area in front of the platforms, into the Booking Hall and through the arch that led to the station forecourt.

She did not look back.

***

"Doncaster.... This is Doncaster... Change here for Caterick and Newcastle."

John folded his newspaper; he had not read a word of it.

He stood up and lifted down his suitcase. He joined the queue of people in the corridor who were shuffling forward to get off the train.

John took a deep breath. This was the end of one journey and the beginning of a new one.

A Northern Tale

Lightning Source UK Ltd.
Milton Keynes UK

171821UK00001B/48/P